Advance Praise

"Allen has taught me to live as if my wishes and desires have already been granted, to be extraordinary rather then ordinary, and to be determined. Allen has inspired me to learn to prioritize, to make the impossible possible, to reach beyond the stars, and to succeed and celebrate every aspect of my life!"

—RACHEL WHITE, judge, *Dancing with the Stars* (New Zealand)

"*Dancing Through Life* is funny, insightful, and inspiring. Allen Brown teaches readers how to listen to their intuition and trust their gut feelings."

—YOLANDA VARGAS, President of the Professional Dancers Federation

"At a time when social media and external 'noise' is drowning out our inner voice, Allen's reminder to listen, truly listen, is more relevant than ever."

—PETER STURGEON, advancing youth through education, mentorship, and love, Boys & Girls Club of the Coachella Valley

"*Dancing through Life* will help anyone who is hesitant to take that first step in their life journey. Allen reminds us that we don't do enough to reach our full potential and that there are so many things for us to discover. His gentle voice is encouraging and inspirational. What a gift to the world!"

—**JEEYOON KIM**, concert pianist

"As a World Ballroom Dance Champion and an immigrant who came to the US in pursuit of broader perspectives, my instinct has always been to live a life less ordinary. Allen has been my mentor since I first touched American soil and has taught me to see and think beyond the possible—to see things not for what they are, but for what they can become."

—**KASIA RYNKIEWICZ**, Ballroom and Latin Dance Instructor and World Ballroom Dance Champion

"This book is engaging, instructive, and inspirational. It is a guide for those who want to succeed on the dance floor or, more importantly, in life."

—**GARY OSBORNE**, Esquire, Osborne & Nesbitt LLP

"*Dancing through Life* truly helped me step out on the dance floor after watching others dance for so long. It helped me get past my feelings of inadequacy and humiliation. I am in awe of how something I used to dread turned into something I like to do daily. Allen inspired me to take that first step."

—**CLARA HAYASHIGAWA**, school counselor, Miller Elementary

"Mr. Allen Brown continuously invests in the future of our most sacred commodity: children. To date, Allen has invested in excess of a million dollars in the Boys & Girls Clubs of Coachella Valley because he believes in the crucial life-saving work that we do. As Allen dances graciously through life, he affords youth the same opportunity by helping us help them reach their full potential, which is the best return on investment we can ever hope for."

—REVEREND DR. QUINTON EGSON, President & CEO, Boys and Girls Club of Coachella Valley and founder of the United States Martial Arts Systems

"*Dancing Through Life* is a gathering of many amazing ideas. What a book! Congratulations."

—YUKI HARAGUCHI, professional teacher, and US National and World American Rhythm Champion

INDULGE YOUR DREAMS &
PURSUE LIFE'S POSSIBILITIES

DANCING
Through
LIFE

ALLEN T. BROWN

GREENLEAF
BOOK GROUP PRESS

Published by Greenleaf Book Group Press
Austin, Texas
www.gbgpress.com

Distributed by Greenleaf Book Group

For ordering information or special discounts for bulk purchases, please contact Greenleaf Book Group at PO Box 91869, Austin, TX 78709, 512.891.6100.

Design and composition by Greenleaf Book
Cover design by Greenleaf Book Group
Cover images used under license from ©Shutterstock.com/createrio

Publisher's Cataloging-in-Publication data is available.

Print ISBN: 978-1-62634-701-4

eBook ISBN: 978-1-62634-702-1

Part of the Tree Neutral® program, which offsets the number of trees consumed in the production and printing of this book by taking proactive steps, such as planting trees in direct proportion to the number of trees used: www.treeneutral.com

Printed in the United States of America on acid-free paper

20 21 22 23 24 25   10 9 8 7 6 5 4 3 2 1

First Edition

Dedicated to Jeeyoon Kim,
inspiration and sunshine of my life

Table of Contents

Acknowledgments

First of all, I'd like to thank my parents. They were one of a kind. They never found fault, and they refused to criticize. They encouraged us kids, and we were totally free to explore and learn.

Thank you to Dick Biehn, who constantly reminded me that we do not have problems; we have challenges. And to Leo Hargrave, a plumber I met in Vail, who taught me to think, to ask, and that "it" is whatever you want it to be.

Thank you to my many friends who helped create Vail, Colorado, and make it what it is today. They were a daily inspiration and taught me a lot about courage.

I have had many mentors. And from them, I have learned that the impossible is possible. And I would be sorely remiss if I failed to include my current mentors. They lead me to new heights in dancing and life: Yuki Haraguchi, Rachel White, and Kasia Michaels. And to Jeeyoon Kim, who always encourages me to aim higher and believe in myself.

Introduction

"... to learn to dance by practicing dancing
or to learn to live by practicing living,
the principles are the same."

—Martha Graham, great American dancer
and choreographer

The day my life began—*really began*—was the day I dared to ask myself a seemingly simple question that started like this: *Wouldn't it be great if I . . .* ? (I'll tell you the rest shortly.) I was seventeen years old. Sure, I had lived a while, but everything else before that day was a dress rehearsal of sorts—important, sure, but it wasn't *show time.* The day the proverbial lights turned on for me and put me squarely at center stage in the role of my life was the day I willed my true, authentic self into existence by speaking a few words. Mind you, at the time, I didn't know the power of the words I spoke. Nevertheless, I said them out loud, to no one in particular. They took the form of a question, which led to another and then another and then another. And before I knew it, I was venturing into a life that I never could have imagined possible as a boy growing up on a farm, smack-dab in the middle of mitten-shaped Michigan's plump thumb.

Over the years, I have come to believe that, indeed, all life starts with a question, with a little wonder, a little *Wouldn't it be great if I . . .*

I believe our true, authentic life begins with this simple question because it signals an awakening to the possibility of *more*. And by more, I don't just mean that there is more out in the world to see, but rather that *we are more* than we think we are. *We can do* more than we think we're capable of doing.

So what was the rest of that million-dollar—or should I say multimillion-dollar—question?

At first glance, it wasn't all that earth-shattering. My mother, father, two brothers, and I were out on a drive. We rarely left our small farm, but for some reason we were driving by Lake Huron one fine day. Oh, it was a sight to behold—just to see the sparkling turquoise blue waters spread out before me. It was a scene that was so different from the one I saw day in and day out, standing on the front porch of our farm. That blue water was simply mesmerizing. Nothing could have been more beautiful, more enticing to my seventeen-year-old self. The open water held the promise of adventure—a life far beyond the farm.

As a boy, I loved to read seafaring books. I became enamored of sailors and voyagers who lived a life that Mark Twain had so wisely recommended to us mere mortals. Sailors threw "off the bowlines." They sailed "away from the safe harbor." They caught the "trade winds in their sails." They explored. Dreamed. Discovered. And I wanted to be like them. I wanted to do just as Mark Twain supposedly said: *Explore. Dream. Discover.*

As I looked out the window and marveled at the sparkling water, I saw large freighters dotting the distant blue horizon. No one else in the car seemed to notice them, but I did, and—out loud—I asked myself *the* question: "Wouldn't it be great to spend a year on one of those?"

Neither my parents nor my brothers replied, but I believe those words cast a spell. They sent out some sort of message to the universe—a message that put a whole series of events into motion. Because within a year, that's exactly where I ended up— far from the farm, a merchant marine on a freighter out in the Great Lakes. It was just the beginning of the first of many adventures that would define my life.

No one would have ever imagined such a life for me—not just a life at sea, but *any* sort of life away from the farm. My brothers were farmers. My father was a farmer. Everyone I knew was a farmer. The high school I attended was just a place where teenagers took a break from their farm chores. It was a glorified four-year stop along the way to a life of working sunup to sundown. Our teachers weren't interested in our aspirations, our dreams, our college prospects—let alone our *questions*. In fact, I would argue, our high school was one of the worst schools in the country. (Though I couldn't blame it all on the school. I played my own part in my desultory high school career.) The only thing I was remotely interested in was counting flies in the library and seeing how long I could sit still as they came and rested on my arms. Eventually, even the flies lost interest in me, thus forcing me to find entertainment elsewhere.

Lucky for me, the library had books. *Imagine that.*

Bored and looking for a way to kill time, I decided to give them a try. What I discovered when I read were worlds and places I had never heard of and possibilities I had never considered until that point. I discovered the ability to question, to wonder, to dream.

I also read the Bible. Not once, but twice. And soon I became so well-versed in it, I was asked to teach at our local Sunday school. Though I was a terrible student, I had a knack for teaching—breaking down complex ideas, helping students ask their own questions, and encouraging them in a way no one had ever done for me. I also discovered there was more to teaching and learning than memorization. The more I read, the more I became curious—insatiably curious. I wanted to know more and more . . . and just a little bit more. I wanted to ask hard questions. I wanted to find the answers to these questions. The more impossible the questions were, the more I enjoyed trying to find the answers.

Long before I saw the freighter that would take me far from the farm, books and reading opened me to entire new worlds and broadened my horizons beyond all previous comprehension. But it was the verbalizing of my desire and wonder, I believe, that was a game-changer. I went from dreaming on the inside to dreaming out loud—and in many ways living out loud too.

A few years later, I found myself at the University of Michigan, where I plunged into my studies in English. Considering that no one in my high school went to college, let alone to one of the best in the country, my being there was nothing short of miraculous. Luckily for me, while I was in the army, several of my peers had taken an interest in me and encouraged me to apply—and to my surprise, the school accepted me.

After finishing college and some other brief work stints (as, among other things, an artificial inseminator of cows), I became the headmaster of the New School in Vail, Colorado. In Vail, where I was surrounded by amazing mentors (including some of the world's most successful entrepreneurs), I soon discovered I had a head for business. Within a few years, I became a real estate entrepreneur in my own right, leveraging several small personal property investments (and a relatively modest stash of cash) into a commercial laundry and an array of rental properties (at one time as many as 200 rental units, which made me the largest property owner and employer in our county) in the then-burgeoning Vail resort area. After I moved to California, I began purchasing shopping centers. And if I had wanted to, I could have retired a millionaire at a reasonably young age.

While amassing a fortune and building my businesses, I passionately pursued hobbies, sports, and creative interests with the same tenacity, focus, and fearlessness I did with my business pursuits. Whether playing golf or tennis, skiing, sailing, or taking photos, I sought to be the best—and that's exactly what I became. I pursued tennis until I beat the tennis pro. I played golf until I beat the golf pro. I sailed until I won innumerable trophies. I took photos until they were published in a book, *Dominion of Shadow*.

But when I discovered ballroom dance (on a whim as my wife and I drove by a billboard advertising lessons), there was no going back. I fell head over Ginger Rogers' heels in love with dancing. I became the three-time World's #1 Amateur Ballroom Dancer. Even now, in my eighties, I still dance. And I have added a new passion to my repertoire—piano.

My recipe for success in all my pursuits is repeatable. In fact, I would argue that anyone can apply the basic principles that guided me in life to their own life. Yes, I can teach you to look beyond the horizon of your current world to a life of adventure and opportunity—at any age and no matter your current circumstances.

My ultimate hope is to teach you that you are never too old to learn something new, to take up a new career or hobby, or be the best at anything you decide to put your mind to and pursue. I believe the key isn't to just keep dancing but to keep getting back on the dance floor every day, mastering new steps, and constantly seeking self-improvement. This book will show you how you, too, can live a limitless, boundary-free life. Whether you're planning retirement or are retired, it's never too late to ask yourself the question: *Wouldn't it be great if . . . ?* It's never too late to reevaluate your relationships and seek a life of happiness and joy. If you're not near retirement age but contemplating a second act and trying to discover a new path or reinvent your life, this is the book for you too.

By the end of this book you will—

- Learn to trust your internal beat (listen and know your intuition), and follow the still, small voice inside you in order to live your life's true destiny.

- Broaden your horizons, and get out of your comfort zone by changing your environment and embarking on a new, epic journey of your own making.

- Understand the power of your own thoughts, and grasp how believing in your own capabilities is the key that unlocks the doors of possibility.

- Adopt a growth mind-set so you can constantly see yourself as a beginner, with a willingness to learn, grow, and constantly improve.

- Decide where you want to go, establish realistic goals, and set out to achieve them.

- Get in the zone and let the joy of the work you do propel you toward excellence.

- Share your gifts and talents with others, and engage in your life with a generous, abundant spirit.

- Overcome obstacles and challenges at any age, and become wiser, stronger, and more resilient in the process.

- Be reminded that, as long as the proverbial music is playing, you should be dancing. You only have one life, and you should live it with gusto.

It is my intention that by the time you have finished reading this book, you will have an idea of what it is you want to pursue, a plan to do it, and the necessary skills to see your dreams become realities.

CHAPTER I

If You Have a Heart, You Have a Beat

"Before you can follow your own drummer,
you have to hear the drummer."

—Srikumar Rao

Through my long life, I've observed other people and heard their stories, and I've come to a few conclusions about the way most people are raised. Like most folks, I was born dancing to the beat of my own drummer. And so were you. We each come into the world the same way—lulled day and night by the sound of our mothers' heartbeats as we grow inside them. The rhythm of the heart is the most fundamental sound. But it's more than sound.

Even if we can't hear it, we can *feel* the beat within and around us. We are born with—and kept alive by—a steady beat. Hold your hand on your heart for a bit and just breathe naturally. *Feel it?* That's your life force pumping within you. There is nothing more beautiful or more essential.

We all tend to forget we have this beat within us—it's where we came from and what drives us. We forget to take the time to stop and listen to our internal beats. And not just our heartbeat but what our heart wants—our inner voice, our intuition. Instead, we listen to what others tell us we should do, what others tell us we should think, and what others tell us we should become. We stray from our own beats and follow the beat of society, the world, our job, our parents. By the time we reach adulthood, our inner voice is all but muted. We can barely hear it crying out to be heard. But it doesn't have to be this way. In fact, we weren't always like this.

Turn on the radio and watch what a small child does. She dances. She moves to the rhythm. Her legs bounce. Her head sways. Her hands wave in the air. She knows what to do. She knows what feels good. She knows what she wants and what her body wants. It wants to feel, hear, and move to the rhythm that she feels inside her from her head to her toes. Her body wants to feel good. It wants to move. It wants, above all, to feel alive and at one with what is going on all around her—a tiny dancer.

Listen to the beat within you

When was the last time you heard music and started to dance, regardless of where you were? How often do you ignore the impulse to be one with the beat within you? If it has been a while, don't worry too much about it. We can change that. And don't beat yourself up about it, either. After all, it's not your fault.

As we grow up, we're told certain things: "No! Don't do that! You'll get hurt! Don't draw attention to yourself! Don't stray too far! Go sit down and be quiet! Don't speak unless you're spoken to! Be polite! Don't ask for too much; you'll sound greedy, ungrateful, and spoiled." We are told so many things that are meant to keep us safe but that invariably instead cause us to hold ourselves back and live our lives in fear.

We grow up fearing so much. We not only fear what our parents will think of us, but we also end up fearing the people and things that they fear. And, of course, they learned to fear those things from their parents and from their own experiences, which often have nothing to do with us.

The result is that we wake up one day and realize we've spent most of our lives afraid—afraid of death, afraid of the unknown, afraid of what others think of us, afraid of life itself. And we've never truly lived life at all. We let these messages of fear become so loud inside our head that they drown out the rhythm inside us. Though the rhythm is alive and well within us from the moment we are born to the moment we die, we can't hear it above all the fearmongering and internal chatter, and we lose touch with our inner voice, our inner beat, which always knows exactly what to do without being told.

Somewhere along the way, we lose the sweet little Elton-John-crocodile-rocking tiny dancer inside us. She's off sitting in a corner, waiting for something to happen—for someone to come along and tell her what to do. But mostly she's waiting for someone to tell her it's safe to get back on the dance floor. She needs to be reassured that no one will judge her, no one will hurt her, and no one will think she's crazy for following her inner beat.

Like our inner tiny dancer, who can no longer hear the music because she's encumbered with fears inherited from somebody else, we are all filled with anxiety because of expectations set upon us by the rest of the world. We were told to go to school or we would never amount to anything. So we went. (It was also the law.) And once we were in school, we were told that the teacher and the books and the lessons were always right.

We were told to stop crying or we would be given something to cry about. So we did. We were told to get married and settle down. So we did. We were told to have kids. So we did. We were told to get a job. We did. We were told to save. We did. We were all very good listeners—to everybody except ourselves. In the midst of what writer and Toltec shaman Don Miguel Ruiz, in his wonderful book *The Four Agreements*, aptly calls our social "domestication," we became cut off from our true nature and, therefore, from our truest and best selves, the selves who have a distinct and unique purpose in this world.

Many of us never even got to indulge in fantasies of what could be or what we might be destined for, let alone ask ourselves what our purpose could be. Fear was instilled early. We were told what the safe options were: "Stay on the farm. It's nice here.

You know what to expect. Every day is more or less the same." Everyone has their own proverbial farm. It can be things like our religion, the town we grow up in, the cultures we are defined by, or even just our families. "Stay here. This is where you belong. Out there is scary."

I was lucky in this regard. Though I grew up on a farm and my world, for the most part, was relatively small, I didn't grow up like most people. I was as subject to the fear-based rules of society as anyone else, but I did have an advantage: my parents. My parents were unique for their time and situation. They weren't religious fanatics or orthodox in any way. We kids weren't threatened with damnation or hell for our wrongdoings, nor were we promised a prize in the hereafter for our good works. I don't think my parents had time for such indulgences. They were busy feeding three boys, which meant taking care of our farm. I was mostly lucky that they were busy folks. They didn't have the opportunity to quell my adventurous spirit, and I was pretty much left to my own devices. There were no limits on my internal beat.

If I wanted to take the tractor for a joy ride, I did. At four years old, feet barely touching the pedals, I steered my father's tractor right over an embankment and crashed it. Safe from harm, I jumped out, brushed myself off, and went on my merry four-year-old way. My father saw the crashed tractor, shook his head, and went about getting it out of the embankment. I wasn't punished. I wasn't scolded or hit. I crashed a tractor and suffered zero consequences. I learned my lesson well enough—steer clear of embankments. I wouldn't do that again. It wasn't until years later that I realized what a gift it was to have such a father. He never reacted with hostility. He never acted out of fear or anger. I wasn't hurt and the tractor survived, so there was nothing to fuss too much over.

With parents like mine, I was able to spend a lot of time running about freely on the farm without any sort of supervision. If I wanted to dig, I dug. If I wanted to climb something, I climbed. If I got hurt, all I had to do was run inside, and my mother, a woman of few words, would put a bandage on me and send me on my way. She didn't censure me with warnings about hurting myself or getting myself killed. She didn't put such thoughts in my head. She let me be, and for that I was—and am, to this day—extremely grateful.

When people ask me why I am the way I am—so fearless and so sure of myself—I like to think my parents had a lot to do with it.

Some things must be unlearned

Our parents, for better or for worse, are our first teachers—our "domesticators," if you will. Their messages—both spoken and unspoken—mold and shape our own thinking. If your parents instilled fear—*Doomsday is always just around the corner, the other shoe is always going to drop, enjoy whatever small piece of joy you have now, because it could all be snatched away in an instant*—chances are you grew up believing the same and living with those fears too. If your parents worried too much about your safety, health, and well-being out of fear of losing you, chances are you felt smothered. They probably warned you about the perils of the outside world and told you were better off playing it safe—marry the safe guy or girl who has the good job and steady income, live five blocks from where you grow up so you never have to meet strangers or anyone new, take the job at the company where your father worked for forty years—it has great benefits and paid vacations.

I am not knocking your parents or even your choices. I am just pointing out that so much of our learning and thinking has to be *unlearned* at some point if we want to have a life of adventure and joy. So much of what we learned as kids has unintentionally shut down the truest and best parts of ourselves.

> So much of our learning and thinking has to be *unlearned*
> at some point if we want to have a life of adventure and joy.

Because I didn't have such a strong external voice telling me what to do and what to think, I tapped in to my inner beat, my intuition, at an early age. I knew what I wanted and what felt good. Feeling good provided proof that my inner voice was working the way that it should. If something felt good—if it felt *right* inside my gut and my body—I could trust that I was making the correct decision. It sounds obvious, but it's amazing how hard it is to learn that lesson. Why? Because for a long time now, our world, our parents, and our religions have told us that if it feels good, it's probably bad for you. Now, that may be a good message to tell people if you want to keep them in line—if you want to keep children's hands out of the candy jar or if you want young people not to have sex with every beautiful person they meet or if you want unhappily married couples to stay stuck with each other until the day they die.

Why would anyone want that? Because that's how *they* were raised.

"If it's hard, it's probably the right thing," we're told. "It's virtuous." But is that true? Has that ever been true? Sure, it keeps us behaving "properly." It encourages us to act like "grownups," like good, obedient soldiers. But is it really true? I don't think so. In fact, I think the opposite is true.

We spend so much time believing that in order to do what's right for ourselves, we must ignore (or even condemn) what feels good. We end up unable to tell when something is, in fact, good for us. We measure everything by the amount of suffering it delivers. If it hurts, we're doing it right. If it hurts, it's good for us. If it hurts, we're on the right path.

Right?

Wrong.

As we know, for example, from dancing or listening to music, what feels right can also feel good. Yes, let me repeat: Feeling good can be good for us. We are so in tune with ourselves and our inner nature when we dance or when we listen to music that our bodies feel light, our energy becomes aligned, and we feel at ease and joyful. Our bodies can do amazing things when they feel good. We can dance for hours, run, skip, you name it. When was the last time you felt good? Really good? Whether working or playing, don't forget how important it is to feel good. That is the true measure of whether things are going well and you are fulfilled in life.

Whether working or playing, don't forget
how important it is to feel good.

Several years ago, I was at the summit's base camp of Mount Everest with a team of other climbers. One of our team, a young man not much older than twenty-five, was in a great deal of physical pain. He could barely breathe, and his body and major organs were shutting down. He was suffering from high-altitude pulmonary edema, which is fatal if not treated. He needed to get to lower ground immediately. But, astonishingly, he refused to. He was hell-bent on going up that mountain. (Talk about being completely out of touch with what is good for you.) My fellow climbers sent me in to talk to him. It took me several hours to convince the young man that the pain he was feeling—the headaches, nausea, and chest pain— could not be ignored or powered through. It wasn't a sign of toughness. He wasn't anyone's hero for suffering more. The mountain would not think him more worthy. The world would hardly notice his suffering in the end. Would his suffering be worth it if he couldn't survive it? There were nobler and better ways to live—let alone die. After some time, we convinced him. He was in such bad shape that we ended up having to carry him down the mountain.

Some of us are so out of touch with what feels good that we're willing to put our own lives at risk in the pointless pursuit of suffering needlessly. We stay in marriages that are terrible and abusive. We stay in jobs we hate. We do work that has little to no meaning for us. We spend our days Googling symptoms of diseases and spend hours in doctors' offices, waiting for the experts to dole out the bad news we know is inevitable. What a waste.

I have never been that person. I have never given much credence to fear and the messages of others. I have instead listened to and refined my inner rhythm. I can close my eyes and let my inner rhythms (or what I now affectionately refer to as my spirit guides) tell me what to do next. I call them, and they lead the way. And how do I know it's the right way? It usually feels good. And so far the spirit guides haven't disappointed me. I would even go so far as to say they have saved my life a few times.

For example, one night when I was headmaster at Vail Mountain School, we got word that a skier was lost in the remote, trail-less backcountry. My partner and I headed out into the black night in the deepest, darkest parts of the mountain. Our visibility was terrible. A major snowstorm had moved in, and we couldn't see anything, not even our skis. But we were determined to find the lost skier. As we were making our way through the backcountry, I felt a tug inside me. Suddenly, the feel-good, confident feeling I had had while moving through the mountains ceased, and I stopped—and just in the nick of time. At the same moment, just several feet away in the dark, my partner got the same feeling and did the same.

When we stopped, we realized we were at the precipice of a steep cliff. Had we gone an inch further, we would have plummeted to our deaths. Thankfully, my skiing partner was just as tapped in to his inner beat as I was. Which goes to show that we all have it. We just have to listen to it, get to know it, and trust that it knows the way.

We are all born with our own inner beat—or spiritual guide or inner voice or intuition, whatever you want to call it. And we should all listen to what our inner voice is telling us.

No matter what you decide to call your inner voice, just remember the most important part isn't what you call it; it's that you call *on it*. And when you can call on it, you recognize it, trust it, and follow it. By trusting and listening to your inner voice, you can become fully alive and who you were meant to be—the person you were *before* the outside warnings, external reprimands, and censors got in your head.

> By trusting and listening to your inner voice, you can become fully alive and who you were meant to be.

Those censors weren't always there. Can you recall a time when they weren't? Think about it this way: What did you love to do as a child? Can you remember what caught your curiosity? Do you remember who you were before you became who you are today? Before you were a student, a son or daughter, a father, a mother, a corporate ladder climber, a farmer, a teacher, a doctor? Before any of that, what was it that made you feel alive—feel good inside?

What would be your answer if you were to sit quietly for the next few minutes and ask yourself *What could I do if I could do anything at all?* Answer it as best you can (it can be surprisingly hard when you're not used to thinking that way), and then pay close attention to your thoughts. Do they make you feel good or do they make you feel bad? Do you find yourself thinking or feeling negative things like: *This is stupid. I'm stupid. There's no point to any of this. It's too late for me. It's silly to have fun. It's an unearned self-indulgence to pursue my dreams. Well, I can't just do anything I want. I have responsibilities! It's selfish to want to enjoy myself. What would the neighbors [my kids, my spouse, my friends] think of me if I followed my inner guide and just did what I wanted to do?*

Or do you find yourself thinking positive things? *This is fun! I can do this! I have so many things I would like to try! I don't care what anyone else thinks of me; I want to try tap dancing [hang gliding, trumpet playing, landscape painting], and I'm going to do it! I was good once when I was little. Wouldn't it be something if I went to Australia? I've always wanted to go there.*

I am not judging you. (In fact, no one is. Most people don't care what you do.) I just want you to take note of your thoughts. Which ones are coming from outside influences? Which ones are coming from your inner voice? Can you tell the difference? If the thoughts make you feel bad, stressed, worried, anxious, or judged, then chances are they are coming from the outside. If the thoughts make you feel free, happy, unburdened, and excited, then that's your true self talking.

There are simple ways you can get in touch with your inner voice and inner beat if you're not in touch with it already. Try sitting quietly for five, ten, or fifteen minutes at a time. Let your thoughts come and go. Don't love them or hate them or block them or ignore them or criticize yourself for having them; just sit with them. That's what meditation is, and it's always been a powerful tool for me. I like to observe my thoughts come and go without judgment. The more you practice this, the more you won't feel obligated to adhere to every thought you think. You don't *have to* believe you're afraid. You don't *have to* fear or succumb to what your parents or friends think or expect of you. You *can* just be in the moment—watching it with a sense of detachment.

The more you do this, the more you will realize that the inner you is the *you* that is aware of the thoughts, but is *not* where these fearful thoughts originate. The inner you exists all the time. The inner you is beyond thought. The inner you is the self that knows what feels good and what is right and peaceful all the time. Tapping into that inner voice and sense of knowing takes practice. The more you do it, the more adept you become.

When you're not meditating, you can still tap in to this awareness. In fact, you can do it all day, every day. How? Be vigilant about your immediate, authentic responses to things, and make them known both to yourself and to others.

So many of us operate out of a sense of obligation, what we think we "should" do. We act this way so often that we forget what we truly want and desire. So get in touch with what you truly want—not what you think others want to hear. If someone says, "We really need you on this committee," but you don't want to be on the committee, don't hesitate. Don't make up excuses. Just decline. Practice doing *only* things you want to do. If you don't want to do the laundry one day and always feel resentful that your partner doesn't do her fair share, ask her to chip in. Or just give yourself a pass. Do something fun instead. Chances are that if you do that, you'll be more willing to do the laundry later anyway. The point isn't just to automatically refuse the bad but to embrace and realize the good. If you do that, you'll no longer feel deprived or resentful or ill-used, and from that better, healthier standpoint, you'll be more willing to deal with the bad.

Practice vocalizing your desires daily, and see if you can tap into more of them. Because the sad truth is that we are all so conditioned to ignore what we want that we often actually have no idea what it is.

Now, of course, there are caveats. If what you want is harmful, destructive, or deadly to someone else, then you don't need to listen to a voice. You need a psychiatrist. But most of what we all want, and what we all deny ourselves, doesn't hurt or cause harm to others. In fact, most of us inflict a lot of harm on ourselves, rather than make another person feel uncomfortable for five minutes by saying the words *no* or *I don't want to*.

If you really want to be able to dance through life, then first and foremost you have to hear and feel the rhythm inside you. If you don't hear the music, you can't do the dance. If you want to live a life of unlimited possibilities, if you want to be able to try new things and explore and live the life you were meant to live, then it's time (to paraphrase what the hippies used to say) to tune in, tap in, and turn on to the beat that is inside you.

Remember, there is a reason why people say "Follow your heart." Because that is, after all, where the beat is. Let the beat take the lead. And before you know it, you'll be dancing.

EXERCISE TO HELP YOU FIND YOUR INNER BEAT

- Quickly, without thinking too much, answer this question: What ten things would you try today if money were no object and you could do anything you wanted? Write them down.

- Look at the list. Are there themes or similarities? What does the inner you long to do the most?

- What parts of your wants and desires have you ignored in order to make others happy?

- What are some things you could stop doing today that no longer serve you?

- What is one small thing you can do today that will make you feel good?

CHAPTER 2

Get on the Dance Floor

"Fairies, come take me out of this dull world, for I
would ride with you upon the wind . . . and dance
upon the mountains like a flame!"

—William Butler Yeats, poet and dreamer

Now that you've learned to be more in tune with who you are
and what you want in life, as well as to articulate these thoughts
out loud to others, it's time to get out of your chair, move away
from the wall, and get out on the dance floor. Granted, for most
people, that's easier said than done.

Throughout my childhood, I kind of did my own thing, but
I often noticed that most people didn't, and it always made me
curious. They got up and did the same thing over and over, and

they did what their parents did, who did what *their* parents had done. Their world was always limited by what was right in front of them. They learned one dance, one tune (which was not their own), and they danced to it from the day they were born until the day they died.

That doesn't sound like much of a life to me. To me, life is like a dance floor. It's pulsing and energetic. It's filled with moving bodies dancing to the rhythm of their own internal beat. And the music is always changing. Just when you think you know the song or you've got the rhythm, the song changes— and it's time to alter your position, adjust your steps, unlearn and undo everything you just did, and start over. And no matter how accomplished you are, you can never predict what song is next or what to expect. You have to be ready to adjust and move to the rhythm. You have to be open and flexible. The next song may not be your favorite. You may not know what you're doing at first. But if you stick to it, or have a good partner, you can figure it out.

As everyone knows, it's the people on the dance floor who are having all the fun. They're engaged and excited. They may have smiles on their faces or have a look of complete intensity, but they are *in* it. They aren't worried about what anyone else is thinking of them. They are completely in the moment. They left the comfort of their chairs and are dancing. They are truly living.

Step out of your comfort zone

I think that besides figuring out your own inner beat, the most important thing you can do in life is step out of your comfort zone and get out on the dance floor. There is an old adage that everything you want is just two inches beyond your comfort zone. Most people never find this out. They are too comfortable with the status quo—or too afraid to discover what is beyond it. Failure? Humiliation? Uncertainty? Perhaps. But what if it's bliss? Happiness? Joy? The love of your life? An amazing new career? A wonderful adventure?

You can never know if you don't get out of your chair and find out. Changing your environment, your orientation, your perspective is the only way to move toward your dreams. No one gets to where they want to go by staying put. Nothing in life ever just comes to you. You have to get up and go. And no one can do that for you; you have to do it yourself.

I understand changing your environment can be scary. In fact, it can be downright terrifying, even death-defying. There are obvious risks involved. Once you agree to change your environment—leaving that chair, that home, that town, that religion, that job, that spouse, that life you've grown accustomed to—nothing will ever be the same again. But what if I told you that everything changes all the time? And the idea that if you stay put, you'll be safe, is just an illusion? Because it is. The only thing that is certain is uncertainty. Sure, you can sit on that chair and watch others dance. But while you're safely staying in the same place, your friends will get up and hit the dance floor, find partners, become extraordinary dancers, and leave you behind.

That's a change. Even though the exciting change is happening to *someone else*, it's also happening to you. The more you stay stuck and stagnant, the more life changes around you.

The only thing that is certain is uncertainty.

And what happens when you resist changes in life? Chances are you become bitter, angry, resentful, and fixated. You want things to stay the same. You want others to do as you have done— stay put. Your life becomes small and petty. And you resist all the changes that come your way. You get old. Your body grows older by the minute. The seasons change. The music changes. The world changes. And you, in all your resistance to change, change too, but not for the better.

The only way to truly live is to embrace change and welcome this uncertainty. Once you do this, you will realize that there really is no better alternative than dancing through life. The only way to truly live is to be engaged and open and willing to take the next steps.

The only way to truly live to is embrace change and welcome this uncertainty.

My life changed dramatically the moment I stepped on a freighter bound for the middle of the Great Lakes. I couldn't have been further from my comfort zone if I tried. The land below my feet was gone. I was both figuratively and literally adrift. When I stood out on the deck of the freighter and looked out around me, I couldn't even see land. My friends and family weren't there, and

I didn't know anyone. I didn't even really know what I was doing. Each day was a question. But I was following my inner beat, and I was learning something new every day.

A similar feeling of awareness must have been imbedded in my mind when I intensely read and reread a brochure on building and flying model piper cub airplanes. I felt as if there was something special about flying.

Sixteen years later, I was sitting in the cockpit of a small plane, explaining to an instructor what I knew. After I finished, he said, "OK, let's go." Not quite understanding, I didn't move. But finally, unsure of myself, I pushed the throttle forward, and we began moving. He said nothing, so I pushed it forward more. Soon, we were flying. Was this the same unknown force that existed when I saw the freighter? I was seeking the unknown. I was scared, but I was taking the first step.

It wasn't always easy. In fact, there were times when I was terrified. *What if I mess up and everyone dies?* This was not an exaggerated fear. I worked in the boiler room. One misstep—adding water to the boiler too early or too late—and the entire ship could blow up. I remember a time when an experienced seaman came to *me* to ask if we should add water to the boiler. It was a very touch-and-go situation. Neither of us knew the outcome. If we added too much or too little, too soon or too late, we would kill everyone on board. I quieted my mind and turned to my internal guide. And, as you may have guessed, we *didn't* blow up the boat and all the people on it to smithereens. In those moments, I learned what I was made of. I learned that I was capable of so much more than I originally gave myself credit for.

You must take risks

Most of us have no idea what we're truly capable of because we've never risked being uncomfortable or scared or put ourselves in a situation where we did not know the answer or outcome. It's easy to be an expert at something we've done our whole lives. I could have stayed on the farm and fixed tractors or milked cows my whole life. That would have been safe and comfortable, and I would have always known what to expect. But I wouldn't have learned anything new—and I definitely wouldn't have learned things about myself.

Yes, change puts us in positions that are uncomfortable and at times terrifying. But most of the changes and experiences don't require us to make life and death decisions. Most of the changes require us to be a little uncomfortable for a little while. We have to be uncomfortable with ourselves—the new self we are getting to know that adapts and changes to the environment around us. It requires us to let go of our attachments to who we think we are and what we think we should be—or who others expect us to be.

So just how do you find the courage to get up off the chair and step on to the dance floor? The first thing you have to do is start somewhere. Anywhere. Once you take a single small step, the next step gets a little easier, and then the next one gets easier still. Start with the smallest step. If you're absolutely terrified, bring a friend along with you. Reveal your fears and ask for guidance and support. If you feel frozen or paralyzed, then you've gone too far outside your comfort zone for now. You don't want to feel overwhelmed to the point of being incapacitated. Don't overdo it. The key is to build momentum.

For example, if you are thinking of changing jobs, the first step might not be to quit the one you have but to start doing some research or updating your resume or even making a list of things you can do to make quitting your job possible. Once you can check a couple of things off your to-do list, you'll start to feel more confident and self-assured, and the next step will start to reveal itself naturally to you.

As you move further and further away from your comfort zone and the places you've grown accustomed to, you will experience some pretty universal feelings—namely fear and nervousness. The first thing you have to know is that these feelings are completely natural, so don't berate or judge yourself for having them. You're no less courageous, no less fearless, and no less capable for feeling nervous or afraid. In fact, I would argue that you are even more courageous because despite being afraid or uncomfortable, you're moving forward anyway. Courage doesn't consist of doing something without fear. It consists of doing something *in spite of fear.*

> Courage doesn't consist of doing something without fear. It
> consists of doing something *in spite of fear.*

Sometimes you will fail

Know that sometimes you're going to fail. This doesn't mean that you're a loser and you should give up. It means that you are expanding your bandwidth of knowledge. You're doing things you've never done before. No one is an expert when they first begin something. Gradually, as you become accustomed to change, you'll come to see failure as a good thing. Failure and mistakes just mean that you're one step closer to getting it right, and you're learning.

One of the greatest outcomes of changing your environment and moving out of your comfort zone is the transformation you'll see in yourself. There is nothing better for your self-esteem than accomplishment. The more you try new things and learn from them, the better you will get. And the better you get, the better you'll feel about yourself. It's impossible not to feel happy, joyful, or self-assured after you've mastered something you've worked at for a long time. And these feelings of confidence will only grow with each new achievement and each new obstacle or challenge you overcome. If you've always seen yourself as a loser or a coward or someone who doesn't try new things, you can let go of that mind-set and start replacing it with sentiments like *I am a winner, I can do this*, or *Every day in every way, I am getting better and better.*

When I was young and started to improve how I talked to myself and how I thought of myself, I started to see dramatic shifts in what I was capable of doing. Developing confidence is like a magic pill that makes all other things in life possible. The more you do, the more confident you become, and the more confident you become, the more you can do.

And this confidence will make you magnetic. It will attract others to you, and it will change how others perceive you. Have you ever seen the first couple step out on a dance floor at a wedding or party? The music is playing. People are milling around the periphery, wanting to dance, but for one reason or another they are hesitant. And then that one couple pushes past those on the sidelines and lets loose. It's irresistible, isn't it? As soon as you see them, you can't help but want to join them. It's as though that first couple, in giving themselves permission to get out there and have fun, gives everyone else permission too.

Before you know it, fifty people are on the dance floor. It only takes one confident couple—one confident *person*—to change the energy of the entire room. No one has ever left a great party and said, "Man, did you see that idiot get out on the dance floor first and get everyone around him to have a good time?" Never in the history of parties did anyone ever begrudge that first courageous soul who stepped out on the dance floor and made it easier for everyone else to dance too.

So don't be afraid to take the first step. Don't be afraid to look like a fool for a few minutes. Because the truth is that no one but you will think of you as the fool. Rather, they will see you as what you are: courageous for doing what it is that you (and they) want to do. And when you do what you want to do, you give other people the permission, courage, and freedom to do the same.

As your confidence grows, so will your comfort zone. Something you may have found uncomfortable yesterday could be comfortable today. Before you know it, your comfort zone is going to be so big that the sky will be the limit and you will be able to accomplish anything. No matter how fearless and independent I was as a kid, I didn't think the world was much bigger than the fence line of the family farm. Then I stepped out on a freighter in the Great Lakes, and my worldview and comfort zone expanded exponentially. And it kept expanding. Pretty soon,

I had crossed an ocean and begun living in Europe and skiing in German mountains. After I decided to quit the Merchant Marine and sailing on the Great Lakes, I needed a job. And a job happened to find me: I became an artificial inseminator of dairy cattle. Keeping a bull was expensive and dangerous. My neighbor's hired hand was killed by his bull, and later the same bull killed my neighbor. Even so, I spent a year with that job, but Uncle Sam wanted me, so I became a soldier.

I trained in Fort Leonard Wood, and then I was sent to Germany. From a one-acre farm in Michigan, I became a world traveler and spent a winter on the European Ski Patrol, skiing in the German Alps. But playing soldier was not my forte, nor was farming.

I found it amazing, yes, but not particularly surprising. When you let yourself grow and expand into a new level of comfort, you are pushing the boundaries of what is possible within yourself. And before you know it, you will realize you truly are limitless.

With this notion of limitlessness, you will soon realize you can achieve anything you put your mind to. And the more adept you become moving—inch by inch, moment by moment—outside of your comfort zone, the more adept you will become at learning new things. Your focus and attention to details will increase. No longer reliant on old habits and automatic responses to the world around you, you'll tune in to your inner voice more. You'll expand the limits of your own imagination of what is possible. And before you know it, you will begin to do and achieve more than you ever thought possible—your life will become an epic journey beyond anything you could have previously dreamed.

All it requires of you is one small movement, one small step in the direction of your dreams—outside of your comfort zone.

EXERCISES TO HELP YOU
GET ON THE DANCE FLOOR

- What routines are comfortable right now? Make list of things you do each day because they make you feel safe and comfortable.

- What is it that you are afraid of or that terrifies you? Is this a reasonable fear?

- What have you always wanted to try, do, or see but have been afraid to? Is there some place you'd like to go and explore? Is there a trip you'd like to take? A new job you'd like to try? A new hobby or activity?

- What small change could you make today to move toward that thing you've always wanted to try or do?

- Let your imagination go wild for a moment. Put no limits on your dreams. If fear didn't stop you, what would you do? Where would you go?

- Now, what small thing could you do today to move toward this seemingly impossible goal?

- What changes have you made in your life that made you feel confident and self-assured?

- What would you regret never trying in life?

CHAPTER 3

So You Think You Can't Dance?

"It's like dance is a metaphor for going beyond
where you think you can go."

—Jennifer Grey, actress and dancer

What if I told you everything you want and desire is completely within your grasp? And what if I told you that all you have to do is change the way you think? Yes, that's right. The key to getting everything you've ever wanted in life is simply changing how you think.

You see, our mind is both our enemy and our friend. We can use it to think horrible thoughts or we can think positive, life-enhancing thoughts. It really is a choice. Learn how to change your thoughts and you can change your entire life. What you think you can do, you can. What you think you can't do, you can't. The mind is limitless; once you can get beyond thinking in terms of *can't, won't,* and *shouldn't,* you can unleash limitless potential.

Thoughts can become things

I didn't, of course, always know this. But one day, while reading Napoleon Hill's *Think and Grow Rich,* something just clicked, and my life began to change. Slowly, incrementally, at Hill's urging, I began to see that the mind has the power to create whatever it thinks about repeatedly. Mind you, this didn't happen overnight. I read and reread this book for years before it really sunk in. Years! And for all those years I was reading it, I didn't see the word *think* in the title. My mind had been so trained and programmed to believe that I needed to work hard in order to grow rich. My brain kept replacing *think* with *work hard.*

So for years I worked hard. I pushed and I pushed. But one day, when I sat down to read the book again, because obviously things weren't working the way I was doing it, I suddenly saw the word *think,* and I couldn't believe it. I blinked and looked again. It didn't say *work hard.* It said *think.* It was as though I had cracked a code I had been working on my whole life.

I didn't have to work hard. I needed to *think* my way into wealth, happiness, and success. You may think I'm crazy.

Because, like me, you have been hardwired to believe that working hard is the only path to success, but bear with me. If working hard brings you wealth and success, then every day laborer in the world would be a millionaire. There are people all over the world who work hard all day, every day—for their entire lives—and never have a dollar to show for it. So working hard can't possibly be the secret to happiness, wealth, and abundance—or anything else you desire.

> **I didn't have to work hard. I needed to *think* my way into wealth, happiness, and success.**

But *thinking* can.

Hill wrote *Think and Grow Rich* at the request of the great steel magnate, Andrew Carnegie. Hill interviewed nearly 500 people, who at the time (during the Great Depression) were considered some the greatest men of the twentieth century, among them Theodore Roosevelt, Thomas Edison, Henry Ford, J.P. Morgan, John D. Rockefeller, Alexander Graham Bell, Wilbur Wright, and W. Howard Taft.

Carnegie didn't want Hill to interview ordinary men. He wanted him to interview men who pushed the boundaries of the imagination. Hill interviewed men who invented things like the light bulb and the telephone. He interviewed millionaires and great thinkers who not only marched to the beat of their own drum, but also were fearless, out of their comfort zones, and refused to do things the way they had always been done. Hill, at the behest of Carnegie, sought to find out what made these men so different from ordinary men. Both Carnegie and Hill wanted to know what common denominator made all of these men so successful. And in the end, what Hill discovered was rather shocking: They had all managed to become masterful thinkers. They controlled their thoughts. They wrangled their demons. They only thought about things they wanted to achieve!

All the men believed that whatever they *thought*, they could create.

Thoughts became things. So if they thought they were rich, they would be rich. If they thought there could be a way to make a car more efficient and faster than anyone else, then they could do it. How? It all starts with *desire*, Hill contends. Or rather, what you *decide* you want. And this, too, Hill says, you have control over.

Some have argued that we have no control over what we desire, but that is untrue. We create desire by what we decide to focus on, and desire is the driving point of all other modes of thinking and success. If you want to be rich or successful, it begins with the desire to be rich and successful.

You might argue, "Who wouldn't want to be rich?" Lots of people! You'd be amazed. The world is filled with people who have either been raised or taught to think that being wealthy or successful is bad, unhealthy, or immoral. They think money is the enemy. This *thought*—this belief that money is the enemy— then becomes a reality. Those people stay poor or are always struggling.

Don't believe me? Look at your own thoughts about money, success, or achievement. Do you hold any negative thoughts about these things? Were you told as a child that it was vain or materialistic to desire things? Most people say they *want* or *desire* wealth, adventure, travel, a new home, a new car, and so on—but their underlying feelings about those thoughts are negative and filled with shame. Their thoughts are contaminated. In the never-ending push and pull between wanting and desiring wealth, and wanting and desiring to be accepted by and approved of by one's family and friends, our thoughts can become muddy, at best. Without a clear statement of intent and clear desire, the things you want will always stay just out of reach.

As Hill argues, it's not enough to wish for something. You have to have an intense, burning obsession—the desire and the thought must be crystal clear.

Although this, too, is not enough. Desire can't get you what you want unless you have a plan and stick to it. Hill offers a six-point plan for achieving any desire—monetary or otherwise:

1. Fix in your mind either the exact amount of money you desire or the goal you wish to achieve. Think of it vividly.

2. Determine exactly what you intend to do to make this money or achieve this goal.

3. Establish a deadline or date by which you intend to make this money or achieve this goal.

4. Make a definitive plan to achieve this goal, and then take the first step immediately.

5. Put the previous four items into a clear sentence describing each part.

6. Then read the statement aloud twice daily, once in the morning and again at night.

The purpose of saying it out loud, Hill says, is to "transmute" thought into its physical equivalent. The underlying concept behind all of this is that the subconscious mind acts beneath the surface to accomplish what it is directed to accomplish.

Or does it?

Our subconscious minds create our reality

We may not know it, but our entire life is determined by subconscious thoughts—all day, every day, our subconscious minds create our reality. Where do these thoughts come from? They are formed over time, during the first few years of our childhood. We are born with a completely clean slate. Our brains are little sponges, sucking up everything we see and hear. What we see and hear then becomes our road map for life. What our parents tell us, what our teachers tell us, what our preachers tell us sticks with us and informs all of our subconscious thinking.

If you were told you were stupid throughout your childhood, chances are your subconscious heard these messages and then directed all of your actions in keeping with this thought. Were you told you were messy? Ugly? Smart? A liar? Funny? Chances are you became what you were told over and over. Now imagine if you were told you were an unlimited being? Or that you could do anything you put your mind to? Or that you were born smart and happy?

The mind is a powerful tool. In fact, it is *our most powerful tool*. It can even heal us. Study after study has demonstrated the power of the placebo effect. If we think a medicine will help us, we begin to feel better. We often even begin to feel better when what we've taken isn't even medicine.

It's not too late to undo your subconscious programming. We can train our brains to think and desire anything we want. Even if you're eighty years young, you can teach your subconscious new thoughts. You can replace old ways of thinking and invite new, more life-affirming, and positive thoughts that will bring you what you truly desire.

How? It starts with *faith*. You have to believe this is all true. You have to believe that attaining your desire is possible. In order for the subconscious mind to act on something, it has to *believe* that something is possible. It doesn't matter how many times you say, "I want to be rich" or "I want to be the best dancer in the world." Saying the words or articulating the thoughts is an empty gesture without the fundamental belief that it is *possible* to do so. Hill defines the concept of *faith* as "a state of mind [that] may be induced, or created, by affirmation or repeated instructions to the subconscious mind, through the principle of autosuggestion."[1] He goes on to say that "repetition of affirmation of orders to your subconscious mind is the only known method of voluntary development of the emotion of faith."[2]

By practicing affirmations and saying your desires and beliefs out loud over and over, you can train and convince your subconscious mind to believe they are true. A belief, then, is simply a thought that is stated over and over again. Eventually, anyone can believe anything.

---

1 Napoleon Hill, *Think and Grow Rich* (New York: TarcherPerigee, 2005), 46.

2 Hill, 224.

That is why if you are born into a Christian family, you believe in Christianity. Those thoughts and ideas are all you know. If you are born into a Hindu or Muslim family, you will believe *those* thoughts when you are taught to believe them at a young age. Most people don't consider or doubt their faith or belief until they are introduced to other thoughts and ideas. This is why religious zealots become so afraid of their children going to school with people from other belief systems. They realize the fragility of their own belief system. It is not so much that the faith or religion is "true" as that its beliefs are based on thoughts repeated over and over again. If you stop hearing such things, there is a danger of losing your religion. Makes you think a bit, doesn't it? It should.

What you think about repeatedly, you begin to believe. That's it. That's the crux of how our brain works. And everything good or bad in your life is a result of these practices. If you allow yourself to believe negative thoughts about yourself, your subconscious has no choice but to act upon and manifest these thoughts into reality. Have you ever met a chronically sick person who only speaks of his illness, his bad luck, his misfortune? Every time you see him, he likely looks worse and worse. It's not by accident. Conversely, have you ever spent time with an avid runner? They're always talking about their next marathon, their next race, their training regimen, and their health. They seem ageless. Hill would argue this isn't an accident either. What you think about and talk about repeatedly, you create. With every single thought, you are manifesting your future reality.

This can be terrifying. What if you think, *I just wished my boss would drop dead a few minutes ago! If he dies later today, is that my fault? Did my thoughts make that happen?* No. Of course not.

However, if you wake up every day and think, *I really hate my boss. I wish he were dead,* and then all day you think of ways to kill him, and you do this for days and then weeks at a time, you will undoubtedly create a situation in which your mind believes that the only way for you to be happy is to rid yourself of this boss. Your mind will start creating schemes. Or you may not be able to control your anger if your boss has an interaction with you, and that may lead to a violent altercation.

So no, a brief thought in passing isn't going to result in something, but if you focus and train your thoughts and desire on one thing in particular, you can be sure that thought will have an effect on reality. When you become adept at training your mind, the more you will see the power of thoughts becoming reality. Spend a week or two being completely aware of your own thoughts. Notice how much of your thinking is negative and how much of it is directed at someone or something. Then note how these thoughts affect the outcomes of conversations or relationships. Make note of any correlation. You may be surprised at how much your thinking determines your present reality.

And now you may think, *But I don't have any control over my thoughts. They just come, and I can't seem to make them stop.* Hill would argue that this is untrue. We, as humans, can exercise complete control over what reaches our subconscious mind, but most of us don't often exercise that control. Expert meditators are able to do such things. They can see thoughts come and go and not become attached to them. They can choose which ones to focus on and which ones to let go. The more you become aware of your thoughts and become aware that you indeed have the power to either tell the thought to go away or to stay, the more you are able to train what your subconscious mind believes and thinks.

Create a clear picture of what you want

Hill believed in using visualization practices. The people he interviewed did as well. Almost all of the people he interviewed created clear pictures in their mind of what they wanted or were trying to create. They imagined what they wanted before they had it. They saw it very clearly. Doing this, Hill argues, cues your subconscious to hand over to the conscious mind the specific plans to make that thought a reality. Expert athletes employ this practice. Before big games or matches, they visualize themselves in perfect form, nailing every shot, swinging the club perfectly, or dancing with absolute precision. They aren't doing this just as a form of wishful thinking. They are training their subconscious to execute the right moves at the right time.

Hill believed that everyone should use this same technique, morning and night. I would add thinking all day—every day—about the life you want to create for yourself is the best training you can do for your brain. There is so much you have to unlearn from your past, and the only way to do so is to replace it with new and positive thoughts. And the only way to become adept at this is to practice it constantly. Eventually you will grow so proficient at controlling your thoughts that you won't be aware you are doing it.

Another point Hill makes in *Think and Grow Rich* that stuck with me is that you must *focus* your thoughts and thinking. There is nothing more powerful than obtaining what he called "specialized knowledge" through your own personal experiences or observations. In other words, you can't become a jack-of-all-trades and expect to be a master of one. You have to focus your learning and knowledge in order to become an expert at something.

Now this doesn't mean that you have to go to school for 25 years. Just because you know one subject really well doesn't mean you'll become wealthy or successful. School alone is no guarantee of success. In fact, you may not even need school. You can gain specialized knowledge by working in a field or just by being around people who are specialized in it. Andrew Carnegie didn't know a thing about steel, but he ran a steel business. He knew how to influence people and inspire people, and he made that his specialty. (He let those with specialized knowledge in steel do their work.) I didn't know anything about laundries, let alone about running a business, when I started my laundry in Eagle, Colorado, which was after I had taught school and then became a headmaster. But I was surrounded by and had access to great business minds all around me. I tapped in to their knowledge, and I used that knowledge to help run my business.

I knew I wanted to do more than be a school teacher. I looked around and saw great men—who were no more learned than me—making a lot more money than I was. The only thing I lacked until that moment was imagination. I couldn't imagine what was possible, because I hadn't seen it before.

And this, Hill argues, is what is holding most people back from living a great life. Without imagination or thinking beyond what is possible, everything stays exactly as it is. Our worlds are as small as our imaginations—or the limits of what we can *think*.

Hill says there are two types of imagination: The Synthetic Imagination and the Creative Imagination. The Synthetic Imagination is what we are all accustomed to. It's our ability to take *existing* ideas and make them into new concepts. Henry Ford didn't invent the car; he reinvented the way it was made. Edison didn't invent electricity; he imagined a way it could be harnessed for use.

Then there is the Creative Imagination. This is our unique human capacity to make something out of nothing. Nicholas Tesla was laughed at for his towers, which he built thinking he could capture waves and communicate over long distances through them. Long before there were cell towers, Tesla imagined a world where we could communicate through "invisible waves." He was seen as a madman rather than the genius he was—and not because he had an imagination, but rather because others lacked one.

Only when we push the bounds of what we think is possible and stop worrying about what others will think of us can we truly tap in to the power of our imagination. Ideas that are generated from our imaginations are the most powerful thoughts there can be. If you want to be rich, or successful, or if you want to achieve any goal, you have to be willing to not only control the way you think, but also to let your thinking run wild a bit. Only then can you tap into the creative wellspring that is in you.

And if you're one of those people who thinks you're not creative or imaginative, well, I don't believe that's true. That's just a thought that you've trained your subconscious to believe. Start telling yourself you *are* creative and you *are* imaginative—and eventually you'll believe it. Tell yourself this for days, weeks, and months. And then when a thought pops into your head that seems crazy, instead of ignoring it or dismissing it, try following where it leads. Imagine if J.K. Rowling had said, "A boy wizard—that's just silly," and had gone about her way on the train that day. Imagine if Edison had said, "Light in a glass bulb? The crazy talk of a madman!" and had gone on his way. Everything from the phone in your hand that receives messages from a satellite in a fraction of a second (from thousands of miles away in space) to the television in your living room to the car you drive to the music you listen to—they all started with a thought that someone had the willingness to listen to and make a reality.

Find a mastermind group

Admittedly, making our wild imaginings reality is easier said than done. Not only do you have to override your own self-censor, but you also have to be willing to ignore the naysayers all around you. One way to help you combat this, Hill says, is to establish what he calls a "mastermind group." A mastermind group is a congregation of like-minded individuals who believe that what we think becomes reality and who also believe in a limitless reality based on an unlimited imagination. Members of a mastermind group encourage and support each other and push each other past their own limits.

In every stage of my own life, I have had a mastermind group to rely on, whether I knew it at the time or not. When I was in the army, the group of men I bunked with would correct my English, give me vocabulary words to study and books to read, and encourage me to go to college. When I was in Vail, I was surrounded by some of the wealthiest businessmen in the country, who encouraged me and pushed me forward. Whenever I took on a new sport or hobby, I surrounded myself with the best in the world. Even today, as an amateur dancer, I am taught by some of the most celebrated and accomplished dancers in the world. Being around greatness makes you great, just as being around mediocrity makes you mediocre. I challenge you to look around your inner circle. Are you surrounded by masterminds? Do you talk about what is impossible—or do you push each other toward excellence and beyond your own comfort zones?

Being around greatness makes you great.

If you want to start changing your life and changing your outcomes, you need to look at who is in your inner circle. Who is helping you to keep the thoughts you are currently having? You can't think big thoughts with small minds. Hill spends a great deal of time in his book talking about the qualities you need to look for in members of your mastermind group, and he lays out 30 reasons not to include someone in your mastermind group. I would argue that there is one basic question you need to ask yourself every day to determine if you are surrounded by masterminds or not: "Are the people I hang around with, speak to, and talk about my life with getting me closer to where I want to go, or are they holding me back?" If they're holding you back, they don't belong in your mastermind group. Move on.

Be decisive

Another aspect of thinking that Hill goes into depth about is the ability to make a decision. The fundamental failure in all people who are either unhappy with their lives or not doing what they want is an inability to make a decision. Without exception, all successful people develop the ability to make decisions quickly. Hill also contends that those who have no desire of their own, who are afraid to act decisively, are heavily influenced by the opinions of others.

All great accomplishments come from courageous and fearless decision-making. And this comes from being very in tune with what you want. Hill says it best: "The world has the habit of making room for the man whose words and actions show that he knows where he is going."[3]

If you find yourself paralyzed by choices or decision-making, ask yourself, 'Do I know what I want? Am I doing what I want?" Chances are your inability to think clearly comes down to listening to anything but your own inner voice. I think deep down we all know exactly want we want and where we want to go. We have just been trained to think of this as selfish or silly. We let

---

3 Hill, 170.

the judgments of others determine even what we dream about or hope for ourselves.

If you want to practice becoming more decisive, start by deciding to *be* more decisive. Tell yourself you know what you want, and then practice stating what you want very clearly. One way to practice this is at a restaurant. Look at the menu and give yourself no more than 15 seconds to decide. Once you start exercising your decisive mind *to be decisive*, every other decision becomes exponentially easier to make. You'll become more in touch with what you want and what you don't want, and you'll create neural pathways in your brain that make decision-making that much easier. This behavior will eventually become a habit.

Hill calls this "sustained effort." You need to build up your thinking stamina and decision-making skills. You do this by being conscious of your thinking in every aspect of your daily life. It resembles living like a Zen Warrior—someone who practices in order to achieve what is called an "awakened mind." By being mindful and conscious of every thought and decision, you make it a habit. You are aware of your first thoughts of the day. You are aware of the thoughts you have while you are driving to work. You are aware of the thoughts you have while you speak with others.

The more you do this, he contends, the more your life will become a manifestation of your desires. However, there is one more caveat to all of this: All the thoughts you think—well, they're not exactly *yours*.

Hill believes (and I believe) in something called Universal Mind or Infinite Intelligence. The Universal Mind is the source of all of our imaginations. This isn't a belief—it is, in fact, a

Universal Truth, Hill contends. The Buddhists and other non-dual philosophers argue that we are all one, and that we are just living an illusion of separation. While our bodies (containers) are different, our minds are connected by and to one universal source. We all have the ability to tap in to this source and create anything—literally anything. Because *if you have imagined it, it already exists.* The idea was generated by the universal source, and therefore it is possible. It's actually just "waiting" to be manifested through our physical forms.

People like Tesla, Edison, Bell, and others, Hill would have argued, were all getting their ideas from the same source. They trusted that source, and they followed it to its logical conclusion—manifestation.

If you put your trust in this Universal Mind, this Infinite Intelligence, your spirit guide will have nothing to fear. You will know your path is certain and that all will be as it is supposed to be. The problem is that most of us have been conditioned to fear things. Fear is our default emotion and state of mind. I would say that most people don't *think* things at all; rather, they *fear* things. They let their emotions get the better of them. However, what they don't realize is that they can control those emotions as well. Fear—and all emotions, really—is just a result of a thought. If you think scary thoughts, you will feel afraid. If you think positive thoughts, you will feel uplifted and positive. It's that simple, but most people let their emotions take over. They don't take control of their thoughts, and so they are overcome by them.

You can't train your brain to think or be open to receive the wisdom of the Universal Mind if your mind is full of emotional chaos—namely, fear. All negative emotions are just a manifestation of fear. If you're envious, you fear there isn't enough in the world to go around. If you're jealous, you're afraid of losing something you have. If you're angry, you're afraid someone is out to harm you. Fear is the leading cause of unlived lives, of staying stuck, of remaining poor. Fear contaminates our relationships and destroys our happiness. If you want to be happy, successful, wealthy, or achieve something, you simply must banish fear from your mind-set. You must decide to trust not only in yourself but also in the Universal Mind and realize that the impossible is possible.

Hill argues that in order to achieve any form of lasting happiness or success, you have to get rid of all negative emotions—fear, worry, anxiety, negativity, and excuses. If you find yourself saying, "I'd write that book if only I had more time" or "I'd have a lot more money if my father had given me a better start in life," then you will never have the things you desire. You are only as good as the excuses you make. If you find yourself making excuses or blaming others for your lack of initiative, you need to stop. You can never have what you desire in life if you are blaming others or making excuses for why your life is the way it is. You are just perpetuating the cycle.

If we think negative, self-limiting thoughts, then the life we create for ourselves is a limited life, regardless of how hard we work. We could work 90 hours a week, never sleep, and give ourselves totally to our work. But if we constantly think we'll never be enough—not good enough, not successful enough—then we never will be. What we think, we create. Conversely, if we think we are successful, confident, competent, and capable, we will be that as well.

What we think, we create.

You can think yourself into the life of your dreams. That's how incredibly powerful your mind is. I know this is a lot to digest. I read Hill's book several times before I actually got it. Hill recommends reading his book three times. I suggest reading this chapter several times too. It is the absolute foundation of all other achievements.

I am living proof that what you think, you create. I went from being a mediocre student to getting into and succeeding at one of the top universities in the country. I had a desire to do well. I put that desire to work every day, and I tapped into an unknown reservoir of confidence and fearlessness that surrounded me. I remained forever tapped into the Universal Mind.

Later, when I was in Vail, working hard as a headmaster at a school there, I looked around and realized I was no different than those that surrounded me. They were no more intelligent. They were no more educated. What did they have that I didn't? Absolutely nothing. We all shared the same Universal Mind. We all had the ability to control our own thoughts. We all had the ability to create our own reality. The only difference was that I saw limits and they saw none. If they didn't like a law, they said, "Well, change it!" If they wanted to buy something, they said, "Why not?" They didn't let their present reality determine their future reality. They also didn't let fear and negativity dominate what they thought about or what they talked about. Once I realized all of this, I entered a zone of no limits. I knew right then and there that I could make any amount of money and do anything I put my mind to.

You may be thinking that, in fact, some things are simply not possible, and that is true. I think this is worth addressing here.

I think we are often so caught up in our ideas of what *others* deem successful and what others define as achievements that we have a very limited idea of what success is. And this stunts our conception of what is possible to begin with. For example, every year hundreds of thousands of people stand in long lines to make their dream of being a singer come true on reality television shows like *The Voice*. The *reality* is that there will not be 100,000 winners. Even if all of them practiced all of Napoleon Hill's steps religiously, not all 100,000 contestants could be winners. I would argue, however, that the majority of the people who are trying out for this dream have no idea what they really want or what their real dream is. They have tapped into a collective idea of what they think they should want. Their thoughts have created an idea that the only way they will achieve happiness or success is by becoming a famous singer. All of the cooperative components for manifesting reality aren't there—they don't truly know what they want, they don't have a talent or specialized interest, and they don't even know where they are going.

Instead, they have put their own future in the hands of "judges"—which is to say, they've put their fate into the hands of others. Note that when I talk about pushing the boundaries and limits of what is possible, I mean what is possible for you and you alone. Each one of us has a certain skill or talent we've been born with. We each have natural inclinations toward desires (if they are not completely obliterated by our parents, religions, or culture). If we tap into these desires and listen to our inner voice, we may see what it is we really want.

I truly believe that we are all called forth into being for a very specific purpose. We have something inside us that is unique to the universe. Only when we listen to that still, small voice inside us can we hear what it truly calls us forth to do and become. Now, when most of us hear this, our first thought is *I can't do that!* And yet that is exactly what you *must* do. You must do what you think you cannot do but you truly, really (if secretly) want to do.

Because that is what you are called to do—not what others tell you to do, not what others think you should do, and not what others expect you to do. But it starts with your thoughts. It starts with tapping into the Universal Mind. It starts with your faith in your own abilities—and an accurate assessment of those abilities. And it begins with allowing yourself to imagine.

You can't create anything that you can't imagine. You must practice pushing the boundaries of your imagination. And that indeed is limitless. What keeps us from realizing what we imagine, or what prevents us from imagining it in the first place, is our negative self-talk, the blocks we throw up in the form of fear and excuses, and the expectations and judgments of others.

Only if something seems impossible is it worthy of one's time and mind. Indeed, by definition, if it seems impossible, that's how you know it's coming from something beyond you.

And that's what makes it something worth your mind to create and manifest.

Starting today, you can begin to do anything you set your mind to. You now have the key that will unlock all other doors from here on out. Believing in your own capabilities, deciding what thoughts to focus on, being open and willing to receiving all possible imaginings, is just the beginning to living a truly extraordinary life—the one you've never thought possible but now realize can be yours, simply, almost magically, by thinking.

 ## EXERCISES THAT CAN HELP YOU THINK ANYTHING IS POSSIBLE

- Make a list of current self-limiting beliefs. (You'll know them by listing the things you think you can't do.) For example, *I can't seem to make any money. I can't dance. I can't swim. I can't seem to hold down a meaningful relationship. I can't get up early. I can't quit smoking.*

- Okay, now we've established what you can't do. Reframe each "can't" statement into a positive one. Keep repeating the statements in the affirmative for the next several weeks.

- Copy the famous Emile Coue quote, "Every day, in every way, I am getting better and better," and place it on the mirror in your bathroom. Say this statement every morning and night for several weeks, and track your results in a daily journal.

- Fix your mind on either the exact amount of money you desire or a goal you wish to achieve. Think of it and visualize it clearly. Write what you see in the journal.
- What steps can you take to make this dream a reality?
- Hill recommends a goal or a deadline. When do you want to achieve this goal by?
- What is one of your most pervasive thoughts that has turned into a belief? Can you imagine challenging this long-held belief? What is holding you back?
- What was something you once imagined but ignored out of fear of ridicule or failure?
- What have you often considered an impossible dream? Now that you know how the mind works, do you still think it is impossible?

CHAPTER 4

Step-by-Step

> "He who would learn to fly one day must first learn to
> stand and walk and run and climb and dance;
> one cannot fly into flying."
>
> —Friedrich Nietzsche

When I was a boy, an older neighbor was helping me chase cattle off of my grandparents' field when he said something to me that I will never forget. It was over 70 years ago, but I still can't shake the memory, because what this neighbor said to me changed me fundamentally. Though I was a boy with few fears or limitations on the farm, where I was an expert, I did have one thing that held me back and filled me with dread: school. I always believed I wasn't as smart as the other boys and girls.

Though I was naturally curious and wanted to learn—about so much—I was afraid to raise my hand and ask questions in class. Why? Because, like most little kids, I was sure if I did try to speak or raise my hand, everyone would ridicule me and think I was stupid. I was embarrassed that I didn't know enough—so I never asked questions, and the loop just repeated itself. I didn't know, so I was embarrassed. And that embarrassment kept me from asking what I needed to know. I was rendered mute in my schoolwork, because I was afraid to admit I didn't know.

All that changed when my neighbor saw me trying to chase cattle by myself. Before that moment, it had never occurred to me to ask for help or guidance. It had never occurred to me that there might be a better or easier way to do what I was doing. But my neighbor said to me, "Allen, never ever be afraid to ask questions." In that brief sentence, he nailed what was holding me back in life: *I was afraid of asking questions.* I didn't recognize it until that moment, but yes, indeed, I was afraid of not knowing it all. And from that moment on, it was like someone turned on a light switch inside me. *It was okay not to know.* It was okay to ask for help. From that day on, I began to do just that.

Don't be afraid to try

To this day, I never let not knowing how to do something stop me from trying to do it. I never thought much about this trait until I was much older and looked around and saw that so few people adopted a similar mind-set. Perhaps they never had a neighbor who helped them out of a cattle jam and showed them the importance of asking questions. I am often amazed at how few people are willing to ask questions. And I am even more amazed by those who use the excuse "I don't know how" as a reason not to try anything new. I have had friends say to me, "Oh, I don't golf. I don't know how," or "Oh, I can't dance. I don't know how." You can't *know how* to do something you've never tried. Most of us don't remember learning to walk. None of us "knew how" before we started. If knowing how were the prerequisite, none of us would have ever walked. You have to start somewhere. You have to take the first step. That step (or misstep—and you'll learn from either one) will undoubtedly inform the next step and the one after that.

I am 84 years young. I am deaf in one ear and have a hearing aid in the other. Recently I had open-heart surgery. *And I still don't let anything—including not knowing how to do something—stop me.* In fact, I am preparing for my upcoming dance competition.

Though I am now an award-winning dancer, there was a time, believe it or not, when I didn't know a thing about dancing. I took up dancing when I was 72. My success as an amateur ballroom dancer never would have happened if I had said, "I'm 72! I'm too old to start something new!" or "I've never danced before! There's no point!" or "I can't hear the music! How could I dance?" No, I never let obstacles stop me. My late-in-life passion all began when I knew absolutely nothing about dance. I was pursuing an interest. I also wanted to do something to stay healthy. I had heard dancing was a deterrent to Alzheimer's and was one of the best ways to improve your overall physical and mental health, so I said, "Why not! Who knows what could happen!"

The only thing that was required of me on the day I began to dance was a willingness to learn and ask questions. That's it. I didn't have to *know* anything. I just had to be willing to be open to the possibility that I *could* learn something new. Of course, I didn't start winning competitions on my first day. When all was said and done, it took me ten years to win. And during those ten years, I practiced every day, because I knew that it was *part of the plan* to accomplish my goal of becoming a proficient dancer. (I also had a secret weapon: my three beautiful and talented teachers, Yuki, Rachel, and Kasia.) To win at competitions, male dancers have to compete against, and beat, *all* other male competitors, including bronze-, silver-, and gold-level competitors on the dance floor. (Women compete against women.) I competed for the first time in 2011. Then I competed two more times, and I came in second in both of those competitions. Not too shabby for an 84-year-old with a hearing aid.

Adopt a beginner's mind-set

I never set out to win competitions. Truth be told, I didn't even know much about the ballroom dancing competitive world. I learned as I went along. And that's how most of us do it—we learn by doing, by taking one step, one beat, one activity at a time. I think one of the best things we can learn is that it's okay not to know something. It's okay to be a beginner. Admitting you don't know everything or that you're not very good at something is one of the most freeing acts you can do in life. Admitting you don't know something frees you from the fear of failure, from doing it wrong, or messing up. No one expects a novice to be an expert on their first day. No one berates someone for messing up something on their first try. We don't scream at babies learning how to walk. No, we clap and rejoice at the tiniest step. When we approach every new activity as a beginner, we are giving ourselves permission to fall and fail. We're also signaling to those around us (if only implicitly): *I need encouragement. I need support. I need help.* And here's the thing: People love to help others. Experts love to share what they know. So *let* them. Allow others to help and guide you.

There are distinct steps you can take to adopt the required beginner mind-set to keep going.

Begin

The first thing you need to do is quite obvious: Just do it. Make the call. Set up the appointment. Show up and be ready to learn. That's it: begin.

Don't be ashamed of not knowing

Turn to those around you and say these words: "I have no idea what I am doing. Can you please help me?" These are powerful words. They invite all sorts of great things into your life. And the more you use them, the more help and guidance you will receive. Do you want to take up yoga? Don't buy all the gear—mats, blocks, whatever—and show up trying to look like you already know everything. As soon as you walk into the room and look around, you'll feel terrible about yourself. You'll be so worried about what others think of you that you won't be able to learn what you need to know to do a proper downward-facing dog without snapping your wrists or throwing out your back.

Don't be ashamed of being a beginner. Don't be ashamed of not knowing all of the answers. Everyone starts somewhere. I'll always remember what my first sailing instructor said to me on my first day. "Allen, today you're four years old." In other words: I know nothing. I am a child. I have no skills. And that is perfectly okay. My purpose is like that of a four-year-old—to learn and have fun. Nothing less, nothing more. And so, too, is yours whenever you venture out to do something new.

Have a willingness to learn

Keep that beginner's mind-set all day, every day. Get in the habit of not knowing everything and having a willingness to learn. A beginner's mind-set isn't just for beginners. Though I have been dancing for nearly 12 years, I still consider myself a beginner every time I enter the studio to dance. And in a way, I am. Every dance is a new dance. The steps are different, the music is different, and I am different. I have to adapt and change on a daily basis, and this requires a willingness to admit I don't know everything. Adopting a beginner's mind-set requires a certain level of curiosity and a determination to find out the answers.

When you take on any new hobby, job, or objective, you'll soon discover that every level of mastery requires a bit more of you—and then more after that. There is always something new to learn and master. If you're not learning, you're not growing. And if you're not growing, the only alternative is that you're dying. Don't die thinking you know everything there is to know. It's not worth it.

Find your teachers

Seek out excellent teachers and mentors who know more about a subject or a concept and can teach the basics of mastery. In every endeavor I have taken on, I have sought out the best possible people to guide me. In dance, I have three expert and world-renowned dancers as teachers. Don't stop there. Don't forget to call on your inner beat—those spirit guides I talked about. They have helped me far more than anyone in this lifetime.

Sometimes, when I have a question and don't know something, I will write down the question before I go to bed. Often I will wake up in the middle of the night with an answer. When I was living in Vail and starting my commercial laundry in Eagle, Colorado, I was going through a particularly difficult time. I didn't know what I was doing. It was my first time, not only as a business owner, but running a laundry as well. Sometimes there would be serious issues that required my attention at all hours of the day and night. And all the while, my beautiful wife, Patricia, was in Denver, dying of cancer. I was bereft. I was out of my depth. I drowned myself into my work so I didn't have to think about the possibility of losing her forever. I couldn't, for the life of me, understand why God was taking this amazing woman away from me. I had no idea what to do in any aspect of my young life. I was fighting battles I had never confronted before. I would cry out, "I have no idea what I'm doing! Please help!"

And an answer would invariably arrive. A solution would come to me. A problem would be solved. And, when there was no way to fix or change something—as in the case of my wife's terminal illness—my spirit guides were able to guide me toward acceptance and peace. Not having to know all the answers, and not having to pretend that I had everything under control, was incredibly empowering and liberating. Sometimes my spirit guides led me to real-life advisors, with real-life solutions that offered me hope and possibilities. Magical things can happen when you simply reach out to others and ask for help.

Be willing to fail

You have to be willing to fail. This is an absolute. You will mess up. You will fall down. You may even hurt yourself or others in your attempt to master your skills. This is natural and part of the learning process. Instead of berating yourself—or worse, giving up altogether—reframe how you think about failure. Decide that failure is good for you. Decide that it is getting you one step closer to your goal.

Practice, practice, practice

Be willing to practice and engage in repetition. Doing something over and over is the only way to achieve mastery. It's also the best way to free your mind. Every time I go out on the dance floor, I think to myself *What am I going to learn today?* I practice every day—the same steps over and over. I do them knowing they will invariably change, and I will too. And I will have to learn something new all over again. The beauty is that with this kind of physical repetition comes a new state of being: After a while, my body knows the steps better than my mind. Even when I am tired, the music carries me, and my body guides me. My body knows what to do even if I don't. Allowing yourself to surrender to whatever is going on around you and letting go of your ego and your self-consciousness is not only liberating, it also truly allows you to begin anew every day.

Don't hold yourself back

Finally, repeat after me: "I am good enough!" So much of what holds us back from doing things we love or want to do is feeling embarrassed or not good enough. It held me back far too long as a child in school. There is no reason to ever be embarrassed about wanting to try to do something that makes you happy—or that makes you healthy or more informed. If anything, we should be embarrassed about *not* trying, sitting on our couches, watching television hours on end, or sitting on the sidelines watching everyone else live their lives.

It is never too late to adopt a beginner's mind-set. Over the course of my life, I've been a beginner thousands of times. Every day, I start fresh. I have applied this beginner mind-set to skiing, golf, flying, sailing, tennis, photography, playing the piano, and, yes, dancing. And I have never taken my knowledge of any hobby or activity for granted. I know that in order to constantly improve, I must greet each dance as if I am completely new to dancing.

If you're serious about committing to a change or doing something you've never done before, adopt a beginner's mind-set. In fact, commit yourself to becoming an eternal beginner. Wake up every day with a willingness to learn something new and constantly improve.

 ### EXERCISES THAT CAN HELP YOU DEVELOP A BEGINNER'S MIND-SET

- What activity, hobby, or new pursuit would you like to try but have been embarrassed to admit? Write it down.

- Once you've identified it, what is the first step you could take to make this a reality? Interested in learning how to dance? Why not call a local dance studio and book a class? Thinking about taking up painting? Make it your business to see if there are adult classes at your local high school or university. Want to read more? Head out to the library or the local bookstore. The steps don't have to be huge. They just have to move you forward. The smallest step will change your reality and lead to progress. Write down the first step and the date by which you will do it.

- Address your fears of not knowing how to do something. Now that you know there is no shame or embarrassment in trying something new, do you think you would be able to give it a try?

- In what other areas of your life could you benefit from adopting a beginner's mind-set, all day, every day? How do you think it might improve your life?

- In what areas do feel like an expert? Is there any room for you to learn something new?

- What mentors or experts can you call on to help you achieve your goals or dreams? Do some research and write down the names of two or three people you think you could learn from.

- What is your plan to practice your new pursuit? How much time do you plan on committing to learning something new each day? Write your commitment down. For example: I commit to writing at least one page of my novel a day for the next 30 days, or I commit to running for 30 minutes each morning.

- Write down and post an encouraging affirmation where you can see it first thing in the morning. Some suggestions are the following: "I am enough." "I have all that I need." "I can do it." Read and repeat daily.

CHAPTER 5

Set Your Playlist and Then Dance

"You're never too old to set a new goal
or dream a new dream."

—C.S. Lewis

Personal goals and achievements weren't something farm kids talked much about. As I said, I went to one of the worst high schools in the country. Most of us weren't given much to aspire to or work toward. (College was barely mentioned.) In fact, I didn't really know what it meant to have a goal until I was in the army. I was lucky enough to be surrounded by ambitious and conscientious young men who valued reading, education, and self-improvement. Though it will forever remain a mystery to me as to why these men took a keen interest in me, they nevertheless believed that I should I go to college. *College? How could I possibly do that?* One word and one book at a time—that's how. The men gave me a word of the day to memorize. They gave me books to read. And then they told me what my first goal was—to pass a college entrance exam and get into college. (I wouldn't have thought of it myself at the time.) With their help, I did just that.

Set goals

Once I arrived at college, I was all on my own. With no one there to encourage me and keep me on track, I worried that I wouldn't be able to do it. But then I remembered the skills I had learned with my army buddies—not the least of which was setting a goal. We set a goal to pass a college entrance exam. We didn't just cram it all in on one night. We broke that major goal down into smaller and more manageable ones. I learned one word a day. At the end of every week, I had learned seven new words. Within a year, I had added 365 new words to my vocabulary. I had also read every book I could get my hands on. I knew what it took to accomplish a goal—one small, incremental success at a time. So when my own first attempt at goal setting came after I got into college, I knew exactly what I needed to do.

This goal setting idea was not to be underestimated. It was

one of the most powerful tools I had. After all, it had already taken me to a place I had never dreamed possible, so imagine what I could achieve if I kept at it—that is, if I set goals for every aspect of my life.

Shortly after getting into college, I decided I wanted to be a straight-A student. I knew that in order to do that, I needed to commit a certain number of hours to studying each day. I wanted to be able to study more than anyone and know more than my peers. My advantage? I needed less sleep than most. So I set up a system: When I wasn't in class, I would study for 50 minutes and sleep for ten minutes. I did that around the clock. I used every waking moment I could to study and learn.

And it worked. I did get straight As. I set a goal, laid out a plan, and then executed it. Years later, when I was in Eagle, Colorado, working in the commercial laundry business and in real estate, I did the same. I set goals each year and then broke those goals down into incremental goals, so that each day I was doing something that worked toward the bigger goal.

Learn along the way

And let me tell you the secret to goal setting: You don't have to know what you are doing. You can learn that along the way. When I ventured into business for the first time, I had absolutely no idea what I was doing. Prior to becoming the owner of a commercial laundry business, I was an out-of-work schoolteacher. I also had some side hustles going on to help pay the bills and put food on the table—carpet sales and a cleaning business. But I really knew nothing about running *my own* business.

You don't have to know what you are doing.

Luckily for me, I had some good, encouraging friends. One of them, John Kaemmer, who owned a restaurant in Vail, was talking to me one day about a problem that he needed to solve. There was no one nearby who could launder all the table linens and uniforms for his restaurant, and it was costing him both time and money. As it was, he had to ship his laundry to Denver—which was a three-hour trip. He said to me, "Why don't you run a commercial laundry? All the restaurants and lodges around here could use one."

And for some reason, that sounded intriguing to me. Maybe it was because I loved to solve problems. Granted, I didn't know where to begin, but that didn't matter. I had a new goal: to start a commercial laundry. The rest was just details, which I could figure out as I went along, one step at a time.

The first thing I did was what I always do when I want to understand things better: research. I looked for books about commercial laundry businesses. But as shocking as this may be, there simply aren't many books on the topic—with the exception of those written for the military.

I started visiting all the small local laundries that serviced nearby towns. Then I drove to Denver and visited large commercial laundries—and employed another skill I had developed quite well: I asked lots of questions. I then went to Chicago and visited laundries owned by the Commercial Laundry Association and gathered a list of all the things I needed.

As soon as I returned to Vail, I started looking for a property where I could build, but to no avail. Another friend of mine, Leo Hargrave, lived back in Eagle, and he said he would help me. Leo had a solution. He had a plumbing building on Main Street in Eagle, and he said he would be willing to add on to it. With no contract between us, just operating on a gentleman's agreement, Leo began adding to his building, with the promise that I would pay him a monthly rent.

At the outset, when I was doing research, all the "experts" in the laundry business told me I that I would need at least $200,000 to start a commercial laundry. But because of the help of my friends and good-old-fashioned farm boy ingenuity, I started the whole thing with just $55,000. I earned that by setting goals and working with a bank that lent me $50,000. I also borrowed $2,000 dollars from my parents, and of course I used my own savings, $3,000.

After I had the space and the capital, I needed the machinery. I bought some basic machines and started doing laundry for local lodges. It occurred to me that I needed better and more efficient machinery if I wanted to scale up and grow my company, so I ordered a huge eight-roller iron that could handle sheets, pillowcases, and table linens at a rapid speed. I had it delivered and then realized I had no steam to heat and operate the machine. That gave birth to a new goal: I had to buy a steam boiler.

I bought a used one in Denver and had it shipped by a semi truck. It was so large that I had to order a crane from Idaho

Springs to lift it off the truck and put it on the slab. When they dropped it off, it was ten feet away from where it needed to be—yet another problem to be solved. I ended up borrowing railroad jacks to lift the massive boiler in order to slide pipes underneath it to help roll it forward. And guess what? They were immediately crushed—yet another problem to be solved. So then I ordered steel rods and placed them under the boiler to help roll it forward. Finally, success! Then, using my own truck, I was able to nudge the monster boiler across the entire ten feet and onto the concrete slab, one careful inch at a time. It took several weeks.

Now that it was in position, I had to put it all together. The only visual aid I had was one picture. And so, piece by piece, I connected the boiler to the laundry. That entire summer I did nothing but assemble the boiler and play tennis. Looking back on it now, for the life of me, I don't know how I did it.

Finally I finished. And it didn't work. So I did what I always do: I asked for help. I called an expert in and realized I had made one small and easily fixed error. Not too bad for a guy who didn't know what he was doing.

Eventually I was the official commercial laundry for all the restaurants and lodges in town and in nearby Vail. And that was just the beginning of my entrepreneurial pursuits in life. It had all started with a goal—to build a commercial laundry.

You have to follow through

Now, the beauty of goals is that they become somewhat addictive. Once you start accomplishing things, you're going to want to keep going. Soon after I ventured into the commercial laundry business, I moved into the real estate business. I had been renting the building for my laundry from my friend Leo, but then I bought it from him. And then I bought the building next to it—and the building next to that. Then I acquired the former Gypsum Train Depot, which had been turned into apartments. I bought a house on Main Street in Eagle and let an employee live there. Then I moved my laundry to a building that had been a former laundromat and dry cleaners. After that I moved onto an acre of land near the end of town and built a towel plant (for the washing, drying, and folding of towels).

It wasn't long before I was the largest landowner and taxpayer in Eagle, Colorado.

I believe there is nothing in life you can't achieve as long as you have a goal. And the more impossible the goal, the better, I say. In fact, almost everything in this world that has ever been accomplished has been attained by people with a goal in mind.

But it's not enough to say you have a goal. You have to be willing to do the work to make that goal a reality. It takes a certain amount of tenacity of will, persistence, and intense and sustained focus. Goal setting is one of those things that is easier said than done. Anyone can say they have a goal, but few have the intestinal fortitude to follow through with the execution.

How many times have you attempted to lose weight, run a 5K or a marathon, or start a new project, and failed to see it through? Setting the goal is the easy part. Saying you want to achieve something is just the beginning. You have to be willing to make the sacrifices, do the work, and show up every day with the goal in mind. So how does one go from goal setting to goal achieving? I have some suggestions.

Understand what's holding you back

If you have not been able to achieve the goals you have set for yourself in the past, it's time to do some internal investigation and inquiry. You may not realize it, but there very well could be a lot of subconscious self-sabotage happening behind the scenes in your psyche. We all have underlying beliefs that have a lot of influence over the decisions we make in life. Perhaps you were told when you were young that you would never amount to much—so on a subconscious level you believe this to be true. Thus, whenever you set out to achieve your goals, your subconscious is pulling the strings in the background, giving you ample excuses why you can't or shouldn't do something. Perhaps someone called you fat when you were little. You may want to be healthy and fit, but on a subconscious level, you feel that being overweight is who you are, and there is no point in trying to be anything different. Most of us are unaware just how powerful our subconscious is. What we tell ourselves day in and day out has an effect on our entire lives.

Take some time to investigate some underlying beliefs that have dominated *your* life. If money is an issue and you want to earn or save more, look at some of the underlying beliefs you carry around regarding money. Do you say things like "There is never enough!" or "All I ever do is work, and I never have anything to show for it" or "I am terrible at money" or "Money is the source of all evil in the world"? These are powerful subconscious beliefs. It will be nearly impossible to make more money if you carry these self-sabotaging beliefs around with you. These beliefs will serve as an escape hatch every time you face difficulty in achieving your saving goals. You'll find yourself quitting by saying things like "This is pointless. I don't know why I bother saving or cutting back on my spending. Something terrible is going to happen and wipe me out financially. I might as well just spend the money while I've got it."

We all have issues from our past that inform our beliefs about everything—money, food, relationships, life, death. If you want to get to the bottom of what has held you back from achieving your goals in life, you're going to want to look closely at what you tell yourself on a daily basis—or what you have been told to believe. It's time to start questioning every belief you've ever been taught and what you have always assumed.

> It's time to start questioning every belief you've ever been
> taught and what you have always assumed.

But not so fast. The self-help guru and writer Byron Katie recommends asking this simple question every time a negative thought arises: "Is this true?" If you find yourself saying something like "I'm so fat, there is no point in trying to lose weight," ask yourself and answer honestly: "Is this true?" Is there no point in trying to get healthy? Can you not think of any counterpoints or reasons at all to be healthy? The reality is that most of what we think on a daily basis is simply untrue. When we say things like "I'm no good at money," we need to look deeply at these kinds of statements and question the absolute nature of them. To say "I am" means that there is a certain permanence to this state of being. Is it true that you were no good at money when you were a child? Have there been times when you made some good choices? Is there a possibility that you could improve in time?

When we start to investigate the truth of our nature, we realize that most of what we believe about ourselves is garbage—self-limiting garbage—that ultimately keeps us, at best, in a comfort zone, and at worse, in a hell of our own making. If I had allowed myself to believe that I was a poor student and couldn't go to college, and I kept thinking that, I would never have been able to achieve my ultimate goals—beginning with going to college. At the heart of all goal setting is the required mind-set and belief that you can do it and that you're worth it. You deserve to achieve your goals and your dreams. Believing this is the first step.

> You deserve to achieve your goals and your dreams.
> Believing this is the first step.

Know your why

It always surprises me when I ask people why they want to achieve something and they don't have an answer. They want to lose weight because, well, everyone looks skinny and that seems like something they should be too! Or they want to make more money—who doesn't?—but they can't tell me specifically why. What will they do with it? What will this money bring to their life that isn't there already? Every year people all around the world make resolutions at the beginning of the new year: lose weight, read more books, spend less money, earn more, and so on. Collectively they all sound the same, and perhaps that is why so many resolutions are given up on within the first 30 days of the year.

If a goal is not personally meaningful to you, there is no amount of motivation in the world that can make you achieve it. If you have zero interest in the outcome or don't even have a clear picture of what the outcome will be once the goal is accomplished, there is absolutely no way that goal will ever be realized. You have to be personally motivated. You have to want it like your life depends on it. I knew I wanted to start a commercial laundry. I saw it as something that would both make me successful and allow me to help people. That's all I needed to start taking action. And these steps are repeatable and doable for everyone—research, ask about what you don't know, make a list of what you will need, find people who can help you, and stick to the task at hand—one step at a time.

Align your goals with your priorities

Make sure your goals are in line with your own priorities. Look closely at your priorities and what you value. One way to assess your current values is to look at how you spend your time. For example, if you say your family is a top priority, chances are you spend a lot time with them. (If you don't, and you say they are a priority, I would advise you to look more closely at both how you *do* spend your time and whether your family really is your top priority.) How we spend our time is a clear indicator of what we value. If family is a priority, they may be a major factor in your motivation. You may want to stay fit and healthy so you can better enjoy your time with them. A priority for me has always been health and wellness. I have wanted to stay healthy as I have aged, so dancing every day was in line with that priority. Aligning your goals with your priorities and what motivates you is a great way to ensure you'll achieve them. Do you value travel? Does it inspire you and fill you with joy? Then set a goal that will get you to your next destination.

Stay focused

In order to achieve your goals in life, you need a singular sense of purpose and focus. So many people try to take on too many things at once, and they end up losing sight of their ultimate goal. It's simple math: The more time you commit to something, the sooner you will attain it. If you're dividing your time between multiple goals, it will take longer to achieve any one of them. To achieve any goal, you need maximum commitment. My advice is to set one goal at a time and go after it completely, with gusto. When I wanted to master tennis, it was the only sport I played. When I wanted to master golf, all I did was golf. When I took on sailing, all I did was sail. When we divide our energy between multiple goals, we invariably become frustrated and disappointed in ourselves. And when we're down on ourselves, we're more likely to quit and fail. Having an immediate sense of accomplishment is the best way to tackle any goal, and the best way to do that is to focus on one goal at a time.

> Having an immediate sense of accomplishment is the best way to tackle any goal, and the best way to do that is to focus on one goal at a time.

Create a sense of urgency

If a goal doesn't *have to be* achieved, it never will be. That's a fact. Without deadlines and an "I must complete this" mind-set, every goal is going to be no more than something on a wish list. Create a mission statement: "I have to do *X* by *Y* date," and then just do it.

Set SMART goals

If you work in a modern office environment, chances are your annual review had some form of discussion around your SMART goals for the year. SMART stands for *specific, measurable, attainable, relevant,* and *time-bound.*

In other words, when you set out to make your goal, it has to be clearly defined. The difference between a SMART goal and an undefined goal is this: "I want to lose 50 pounds by cutting

200 calories a day and working out for one hour a day six days a week (specific and measurable) in order to improve my overall health (relevant) in one year (attainable, time-bound)" versus "I want to lose a ton of weight this year" (non-specific, unmeasurable, unattainable, neither relevant or time bound). In order for something to be measurable, numbers have to be attached. Even if something doesn't at first appear measurable, find a way to make it so. "I am going to write a book" becomes "I am going to write a 300-page book by getting up at six o'clock every morning, walking into my office, and writing for one complete hour until one page is written (specific, measurable) for the next 300 days (time-bound, attainable) to see my lifelong dream of writing a book become true (relevant)." Many people fail because their goals miss one or more of these steps.

Some goals are simply unattainable and set people up to fail. Some people say, "I am going to make a million dollars this year." That's specific, but is it attainable if you're making fifteen dollars an hour? If making a million dollars is a nonnegotiable goal and you're hell-bent on it, then you may want to adjust your timeline, change your specifics, or even evaluate its relevancy by asking, "Will this goal really enhance or improve my current life?" Asking yourself "Why do I want to achieve this goal" and "Is this true?" will help you evaluate its relevance.

Externalize your goals

The moment I said *out loud* to my friends that I indeed wanted to go to college, I set into motion powerful forces that were beyond my comprehension. We externalize our goals by putting them out into the universe. In so doing, we make our thoughts into something more than thoughts. When we take this a step further and write it down, we make the goal real. When we tell others about our goals, we are then under obligation to do something about it. Someone will invariably ask us about what we're doing. I do have one caveat: Don't tell just anyone. My advice is to only tell people who genuinely care about you and want to see you succeed. It's important to surround yourself with people who will constantly encourage you on your journey. The world is filled people who enjoy bringing others down. Avoid them at all costs and by no means tell them your goals. There is nothing worse than being excited about the prospect of achieving a goal and hearing someone you love say that it's a stupid idea or a fool's errand. Don't let others' lack of self-motivation or self-discipline destroy your dreams.

Post your goal where you can read it every day

Just as you did with positive affirmations, write down your goal and post it where you can see it every day. Your goal should never be far from your mind. It should guide all of your daily decisions. When you have a goal, you suddenly have a very clear purpose and reason for being. If your goal is to run a marathon, then running every single day is going to be a priority. That means you will probably need to run before you go to work. Therefore, if a friend asks you out for drinks at night, you will most likely decline. Why? Because if you drink at night, you can't wake up and run the next day, and if you can't get up and run and reach your weekly mile goals, then you won't be prepared for your marathon. Having a reminder of your goals where you can see them is imperative in the beginning when you are still forming those habits. Once you have a routine down, having the goal top of mind will be less of an issue, but it is still valuable to have it written down where you can see it from time to time, especially when you need a boost.

Don't give up

Nothing worth having or achieving happens overnight. In fact, our sense of reward and accomplishment is directly related to the amount of time and effort we put into whatever it is we wanted to achieve. It is so easy to get frustrated and want to throw your hands up when working toward a goal, especially when things are challenging or difficult. Let me assure you, there has never been a straight line to success. Every person who has achieved anything knows struggle, failure, and seeming defeat. You are going to have days when you feel like it is impossible to go on. This is absolutely normal. The key is to remember that this is just part of the process. You can't give up. You can never, ever give up on your goals and dreams. You can take a step back, reassess, realign, or change your strategy, but once you set a goal that you feel you *have* to do, then you have to dig in and go for it.

Simply put, decide where you want to go, set realistic goals, set out to achieve them, and don't let anyone, including yourself, stop you!

EXERCISES THAT CAN HELP YOU
SET AND ACHIEVE YOUR GOAL

- What goals have you set in the past and failed to achieve? What self-sabotaging beliefs or behaviors have held you back?

- What is your why? What motivates you and drives your actions?

- What is a major priority for you? Money? Travel? Family? Health? Does the time you spend in these areas reflect the truth of your statement?

- Decide on one goal you would like to achieve in the next six months to a year. Write a book? Climb a mountain? Run a 5K? Take a world-class vacation? Does this goal align with your priorities? Look at the entire scope of the project and then break it down into achievable daily goals. For example, if you want to write a 200-page book in the next six months, all you have to do is write a little more than a page a day. The average person can write a page in about hour. Can you allot an hour of your day to writing for the next six months? If you need $6,000 dollars to take that trip of a lifetime, can you put away $500 dollars a month over the next year? That's $125 a week. Is there something you can cut back on or some way to earn $125 extra a week to do so?

- Who will you tell about your goals? Name one or two people who you know will support and encourage you.

- Write a note from your future self (one year from now) to your current self. What goals has this future self achieved? What is your life like? What are you doing? What encouragement and advice does your future accomplished self have for you? Date it, put it aside, and read it one year from now. You may be surprised to see all that you've actually accomplished.

CHAPTER 6

The Rhythm Is Going to Get You

"Those who flow as life flows know they
need no other force."

–Lao Tzu, philosopher

Over the years, I have had firsthand experience being in *flow*—where I could dance for hours and let the music take me and not feel an ounce of pain or even notice the passing of time. And I have been able to witness flow in action as well. I have been blessed to work with world-class dancers capable of doing forty dances, one after the other, nonstop. What would physically exhaust the average person, these highly trained, practiced, and elite dancers can do effortlessly because they are at one with the music and thoroughly enjoy what they are doing.

When you can disconnect from the world (and from yourself) and become completely immersed in an activity you enjoy, the hours just slip by. Flow makes our best work possible, and I believe it is responsible for our happiness. When we're in flow, magic just seems to happen. And when we're out of it? Things feel like a struggle. Think of a time you were in flow—when time disappeared because you were doing what you loved. What was it that you were doing? How does it affect your performance when you're in flow? And conversely, what's it like to perform things when you're out of flow (i.e., stuck in your own mind and thoughts)? Do you struggle? Overthink? Mess up?

You're not alone. In fact, I sometimes use my knowledge of how flow works to my advantage in sports. When I am playing with highly accomplished golfers who seem to be in the zone or in flow, I know to dominate them by messing with them and getting them to snap out of flow. It's quite simple, really: I take them out of their body and make them *think* instead. Once, when I was playing with an expert golfer, I asked him a question just as he was about to swing. "Do you always put your thumb like that?" Until that moment, the golfer hadn't thought about his thumbs. By being taken out of the moment and prodded to overthink the process, he was unable to play well the rest of the day. This proves my point. Most of us don't realize that by overthinking, we get in our own way. Overthinking stops the momentum. More often than not, overthinking keeps us from starting in the first place.

Learn to achieve flow

Becoming one with the music or rhythm of your life and learning to go with the flow is the key to not only accomplishing life's goals, but also to enjoying life. In order to achieve flow, though, you need application, repetition, and frustration. It's like the old joke:

> A tourist in New York City stops an old man on the street.
>
> Tourist: How do I get to Carnegie Hall?
>
> Old man: Practice!

Exactly. *Practice, practice, practice.* After sufficient practice, any activity becomes effortless. By being one with the movement, body, breath, and intuition, you become inseparable from the activity and enter a state of flow.

Flow is a by-product of intense and singular focus. While it's great to have a number of goals and start each day off with a list of things to accomplish, if you're always focused on the next thing to do, it will be nearly impossible to achieve flow. Flow requires a present state of mind. It requires being centered in the understanding that there is no past, no future—only now. Flow can't happen with 20 tabs open on your computer and constant interruptions. Flow can't happen if you're multitasking, trying to do four or five things at once.

Flow requires a present state of mind.

If you want to achieve flow, you have to be willing to let go of some things—the sense of controlling time, checking off 20 things on a daily to-do list, or answering every email or text that comes your way in a day. To be in flow means to be so intensely focused that nothing else matters—not even eating. Most people who are in a state of flow often forget to eat altogether.

I realize that this is all easier said than done. While flow is a seemingly effortless state of being, getting to it requires several steps.

Eliminate what you hate to do, and do more of what you love to do

This may seem like a no-brainer, but doing what you love really is the most essential and foundational element of flow. That's why the saying is not "Time flies when you're miserable!" When you hate every minute of what you're doing, you watch clocks—and the hands never seem to move. It's impossible to feel momentum. All you can manage to do is think about how much you hate what you're doing. Conversely, when you're having fun, time flies. *Whoa? Did that night of dancing just happen? Is that concert really already over? I didn't want that book to end!* The more you dread doing something, the more difficult it will be for you, not only to begin but also to be in flow. So if you're committed to a job, hobby, or even a relationship that seems like the seventh circle of hell with no way out, I would take a moment to reevaluate your life choices. You have one life. Do you really want to be miserable—a clock-watcher—for your remaining days? What brings you joy? What sets your soul on fire? What can't you wait to do? Whatever the answer to that question is, that's the thing you should be doing to enter flow.

Practice presence of mind

Our brains are miraculous. They can generate 60,000 thoughts a day, most of which we have absolutely no control over. What we do have control over is what we do with these thoughts. Do we hold on to them? Ruminate over them? Let them run amok? Do we let them hijack our moods—and our day?

I am a huge proponent of meditation. Spending time in observation of your own thoughts and not attaching any judgment to them (as a bad thought or a good thought), but instead witnessing them and releasing them is excellent practice for training your neural pathways. The more you sit in silence and focus with intention on your own breath, the more you will be able to train your brain to stay on task. And the more it can stay on task, the less derailed it will be by all the thoughts that float to your consciousness each day. I recommend starting with five or ten minutes a day and working your way up to sitting for an hour. There are lots of free apps that can help you meditate and focus. One of the best ones is Insight Timer. It provides thousands of meditation practices, each with a set amount of time and for a specific topic. If focus is something you want to work on, there is a meditation for that. Give it a try for a few weeks and see if the chatter in your brain seems to quiet down.

The more you sit in silence and focus with intention on your own breath, the more you will be able to train your brain to stay on task.

Choose things that challenge you and push you beyond your comfort zone

When we do things on autopilot—like driving to work or eating an entire bag of potato chips while watching reruns—we are not in flow. We're unconscious. Feeling numb and out of it is not the same thing as being in flow. To be in flow, you have to be conscious of what you're doing. Your brain has to be fully focused on the task at hand. When we are engaged in challenging acts, we are working our brain. We are creating new neural pathways. And when we repeat these activities over and over, our brains learn how to do things with little effort. Pick a task that you love but challenges you and forces you to be "awake" (i.e., fully present and engaged). This is where practice comes in. The more you practice and take on a difficult concept or skill, the more likely you will be able to sustain focus.

Find your optimum work time

This is crucial. Not all people have the same circadian rhythms. We all have optimum sleep and wake cycles and hours of the day when we are most alert and productive. The old saying "The early bird gets the worm" rarely holds true for night owls. Not everyone is built the same way. Working with your body's natural rhythm is the key to achieving flow. Having a consistent schedule—a time in which you show up every day at the same time that works best for you—all but ensures that you'll be able to achieve flow.

> Working with your body's natural rhythm is the key to achieving flow.

Work in your optimum space

Some people need absolute quiet to work. Some people enjoy a bit of white noise. Some people are inspired by their own clutter, pictures, sentimental tchotchkes, and books in their workspace, while others can become completely overwhelmed and stressed out by so many distractions. It's all about personal preference. Only you know what helps you feel at ease. And that is the goal— to create a comfortable place where *you* feel calm. Feeling stressed out, overwhelmed, or frantic is the opposite of what you want when trying to achieve flow. Some activities—especially those that take place outdoors—lend themselves to helping you feel calm, comfortable, and at ease.

Set a time limit (at first)

Once you've become accomplished at achieving flow, this will be less of an issue. You'll be able to work for hours and hours— working through lunchtimes, alarms going off, and ignoring distractions that would bother most people. However, in the beginning, when you're learning to achieve a state of flow, you have to give yourself a set amount of time to work toward. That means scheduling a reasonable set of time—just one or two hours—for a task at hand and sticking with it until you can work up to a longer time.

Keep at it

As I said earlier, practice, practice, practice. Every person I know who achieves flow is able to do so because they engage in the same beloved activity over and over again. I am able to dance for hours at a time now because I put consistent time in, over and over.

Let go and surrender to the moment

One of the best parts of being in flow is the moment you can just let go and be completely at one with the activity. This takes practice. As humans, we love to control outcomes. We love to have an idea how something *should* be. There is nothing wrong with that—usually. However, when you're in a state of flow, you have to be willing to let go of how you think things should be. You have to allow yourself to be surprised by what you discover. You'll be amazed to discover what you are able to do when you just let go and let the rhythm of life move you forward.

> When you're in a state of flow, you have to be willing to let go of how you think things should be.

I promise you that if you follow these steps, it won't be long before you'll start seeing results. Besides feeling the joy and pleasure of being in flow, you'll start to see your entire life transform. By being fully engaged and happy in the work you do, you'll notice your mood improve, which is a natural by-product of feeling accomplished and productive. You'll become more alert and awake in your other activities as well, because your brain will be operating more efficiently, with focus, calm, and ease. You'll also notice your tolerance for those activities that bore you to death will wane. Soon you will find yourself avoiding them altogether, choosing instead more positive and flow-inducing activities.

As you become adept at achieving flow, you'll notice your relationships change too. It's amazing how feeling happy, joyful, confident, and positive can impact not only your own energy, but the energy of all those around you.

One of the greatest joys and gifts of life is being able to use your God-given skills and talents. You truly begin to live when you are able to develop these talents in such a way that they delight and inspire others.

We are *supposed* to be happy. We are *supposed* to be joyful. The work we do and the activities we engage in should delight us. When we are happy using our talents, we spread that joy, love, and energy outward. We pour it into the world and make it better. Suffering, doing things you hate, and struggling at meaningless tasks (being busy for the sake of being busy) aren't doing you or the world any favors.

Dance. Sing. Play the piano. Listen to your favorite albums. Write poetry. Garden. Sail. Hike. Cook. Act. Run. Do yoga.

Knit. Paint. Sculpt. Travel. Whatever it is you choose to do, do it because you love it. It won't take you very long to see the amazing benefits of giving time to the things you most love. And more importantly, you'll begin to see that joy is the true path to excellence and a life well lived.

EXERCISES THAT CAN HELP YOU GET INTO THE FLOW STATE

- What activity do you engage in currently where time just seems to disappear? Listening to music? Playing music? Doing yoga? Dancing?

- How much time do you dedicate to the activities that you love to do? Do you feel like it is enough?

- If you can't think of an activity you love that you're currently engaged in, think back to your childhood. When did you have the most fun? Is there a chance you can start something similar now?

- What skills or talents would you like to develop and spend time practicing so you can achieve a state of flow?

- What are some areas of your life that are busy but bring you zero joy or fulfillment? What can you do to stop doing those things altogether?

CHAPTER 7

Honor Your Partner; Honor Your Corner

"Prayer does not use up artificial energy, doesn't burn up any fossil fuel, doesn't pollute. Neither does song, neither does love, neither does the dance."

—Margaret Mead, author

One of the greatest things about ballroom dancing is that you need a partner to succeed. And you're only as good as the person with whom you're dancing. And more often than not, your partners make you better. In partnerships, sometimes you give and sometimes you receive. That is what partnership is all about. And this, my friends, is what life is all about too. There would be no point to any of my success in life if it all were just for me. It would feel hollow. I am a firm believer in the adage "To whom much is given, much is expected." I have been on the receiving end of so much kindness, mentorship, support, and love in my life that it is only fair that I give the same away. So many of the people I am indebted to for my own success are no longer around, so the only thing I can do is pay it forward and hope that others will do the same long after I am gone.

Over the years, I have donated over a million dollars to foundations such as the Girls and Boys Club in Mecca, California, because I care deeply about their mission. As a child who grew up affected by a poor educational system, I feel strongly about investing in the education of children who are growing up in destitute areas. I personally know what it is like to grow up on the margins of society and feel that I, as a child, was nothing more than an afterthought. I not only know what it does to a child psychologically, but I also know how it puts children at a serious socioeconomic disadvantage for their entire lives. Now, some may argue that I turned out all right despite my poor education. And that's true. But not everyone with a bad education, like mine, has the unusual advantages I've had.

I have been incredibly lucky. I can't tell you how many times a person came along and pointed me in the right direction or helped pull me along on my path. I was always surrounded by incredibly generous souls who wanted to bring out the best in me. First it was my family, then it was the guys in the Merchant Marine, then it was my army buddies, then it was my professors in college, and then it was all the brilliant and intrepid entrepreneurs in Vail and Eagle—and after that, it was every expert and mentor I hired to help me along the way. No one gets to where they are in life without others. If you think otherwise, you might want to spend some time looking back over your past. Locate a memory that points to a successful moment in your life, and then reach all the way back to how it all got started. Chances are there was a person there helping you along.

Give back; pay it forward

There are a lot of negative people in the world who walk around with a chip on their shoulders, saying things like "I had no help, so why should anyone else get a leg up?" Nonsense. You're not thinking hard enough or remembering correctly. If you have ever had a job, someone hired you. They didn't have to hire you. You may think you worked hard and earned that position, and maybe you did. But I am here to tell you that for every one of you who works hard and is talented, there is another guy who thinks the same and is every bit as deserving of the same position. So thank that person who took a risk on *you*. Thank the teacher who encouraged you or taught you. Thank your parents for teaching you the values you have now. Or if they were basically rotten and you have nothing good to say about them, thank them for showing you what you didn't want to be. Then think instead of the person who taught you how to be a good or noble person. I bet you didn't figure that out on your own.

My point is that we all have someone we're in debt to. It's not very American to think this way, I know. We like to believe that we all walked out of our mother's womb on our own volition, bathed and fed ourselves from day one, checked the NASDAQ before we entered the first grade, and got to where we are today by "pulling ourselves up by our bootstraps." But that's a load of bunk. Most of us aren't even aware of the outside help we got along away. There are so many silent angels all over our world, doing quiet, generous work without us even knowing about it.

I know that most of the kids who benefit from the amazing resources of the Girls and Boys Club in Mecca have no idea who I am. I realize many don't know that the money I gave helped to hire a coach that made a difference in their lives or paid for the space that gave them a safe place to go after school. I'd like to think that at least one life was changed by the Girls and Boys Club, and that person grew up to be someone who gives back now and continues the cycle of giving. Because that is what is going to save not only ourselves, but the world we live in today.

Giving back and paying it forward doesn't have to be something only those with money to spare do. There are an infinite number of ways to give without having millions of dollars in the bank. In addition to supporting the Girls and Boys Club, I like to support the arts. I am especially committed to helping others continue in their craft. I believe art—music, dance, painting, sculpture, photography, acting, writing, you name it—saves the soul. These are noble pursuits that don't always pay well. We need a world that creates rather than destroys, and artists are the great creators, the great peacemakers, the great saviors of our world. Support local artisans. Buy local; attend art shows, concerts, movies, and local high school plays. It doesn't have to be a major event. Just get out there and find ways to help and give back to others whose talents and gifts have brought so much joy to you.

I can think of nothing more healing and uplifting than listening to beautiful classical piano played by a pianist who feels the music throughout her entire body and soul. Art has the power to transform even the most hard-hearted among us. I have never hesitated to support artists. I see it as a way of giving back to them for all the joy they have given me over the years.

But there is another way to give back as well—with your own talents and artistry. I see my writing, my photography, and my dancing as gifts as well. Bringing joy to others is a gift in and of itself.

At some point, your talents and gifts have to be externalized and given away. Each of us is put here on earth with a unique skill or talent, and it is part of our purpose to give that away in the service of others. The key to abundant, prosperous, and joyful living is giving and being generous of spirit.

> The key to abundant, prosperous, and joyful living is giving and being generous of spirit.

We all know we didn't get where we are today without the help and mentorship of others. Showing gratitude is the first step in abundant living. The second step is to pay it forward and give it all away. You may wonder, though, if you give everything you have away, what will you have left? I am here to say the magical part of giving is that what we give away, we always get back. The key to happiness is having a spirit of generosity, so bow to those who help you, and bow to those who follow.

I truly believe I would not be the person I am today if it were not for all the generosity of others along the way. And now it is my turn to give back. You can give back, too—and it doesn't have to be in the same way. There are so many ways to give. Here are some tips to help you get started.

Understand what matters to you

In order to know how to allocate time or money, you have to know what matters to you and what is truly a priority in your life. Education and children matter a great deal to me because of my own experiences—so that is where I invest my money. The arts have given so much to me as well, and I have seen how wonderfully society benefits when we contribute to the arts. Take some time to consider what truly matters most to you and what you are passionate about. Consider the organizations that helped you or friends or family members in the past—they are good places to invest, because you know their efficacy. If you care about animals, perhaps there are local shelters you can donate to. If you don't have the money to give, could you donate an hour a week volunteering, or could you become a foster caregiver to the animals? It doesn't have to be earth-shattering, overly time consuming, or expensive to give. Once you put yourself out there to give what you can, you'll realize how much need there is and what a huge difference even the smallest amount of generosity makes.

Understand that what you give away comes back

One of the major reasons people give me for not volunteering their time or donating their money is they don't have enough of either. You know my great enthusiasm for the book *Think and Grow Rich*; it made me a true believer in the notion that what we think becomes a reality. I believe it in the most literal sense. If we think we don't have enough time or money, we will *never* have enough time or money, and that is all we will ever experience in life—lack, insufficiency, need. There will never be enough.

This is scarcity thinking. And scarcity thinking is what keeps people in deep dark holes in life—yes, more than anything someone else could say or do to them. If you want to live an abundant life, where time and money are not an issue, you must change your mind-set and believe you already do have enough time and money. In fact, you should walk around thinking and saying things like: "I have all that I need." This statement is powerful and transformative. With it you will soon realize that you do indeed have all that you need—and, in fact, that you have plenty to share and spare.

And here's the beauty of this abundant thinking: It's limitless. The more you give away, the more comes back to you. The more time you give in the service of others and the more money you give away to help others, the more will come back to you. The universe works this way. I know this for a fact because I have seen evidence of it in my own life. And I have seen the evidence in others' lives. Look around you—look at the chronic complainers, the cheapskates, the woe-is-me-ers, the ones who never seem to have enough time for anyone else but themselves. Look at them and ask yourself: Are they happy? Abundant? How is that way of life working for them?

Those same people are usually bogged down in drama, beset by one problem after another, and are quite simply no fun to be around. Their lives are a direct result of their scarcity thinking. If you want to truly live a generous, happy, and abundant life, then you have to start giving. You have to give with joy and love. You have to give money and service, all the while trusting that it all comes full circle.

Make a gratitude list

If you truly want to understand where you came from and why you are the way you are, you have to be willing to get outside yourself and take some time to recognize all the people who got you to where you are today. There is nothing more uplifting and beneficial to your mood and overall well-being than taking the time to sit down and list all the people, things, and events you are grateful for.

> There is nothing more uplifting and beneficial to your mood and overall well-being than taking time to sit down and list all the people, things, and events you are grateful for.

This practice has never failed me. Whenever you're feeling down or want to throw yourself a pity party for all the things not going your way in life, I suggest getting out a piece of a paper, grabbing a pen, and writing down all the things you have going for you. If you're particularly low, then start small. It might be something like "I woke up today" or "I have two legs that still work" or "I can still read, and I enjoy that." If you try hard, you will find something in this life to be grateful for. Then move on to people. What people are you thankful for in your life? Even if you are all alone and your children have deserted you and your husband was a no-good lout, is there someone, anyone, who was kind to you? Was there a cashier at the grocery store who smiled at you or someone who opened the door for you?

A funny thing happens when you focus on the good stuff, the kind people, and the things that are going right in life—you get more of those things. The more you focus on positive things and things you're grateful for, the more you'll start seeing more of those things in your own reality. The power of gratitude doesn't just change you internally; it changes your external reality as well. The more gracious and grateful you are to others, the more grace and gratitude you will receive in your own life.

And you may need to start with yourself. So many of us are hardest on ourselves. We beat ourselves up. Say thank you to your younger self, who got you to where you are today. Say thank you to your present-day self for doing the best you can. The more love and gratitude you give yourself, the more you will be able to shine it outward toward others—and the more willing you will be to receive it when it all comes flowing back to you.

Now pay it forward

If you have something to be grateful for, then you have someone to thank. However, I realize that all of us have people in our lives that we will never be able to pay back or thank in person. Most of us aren't even conscious of the kindness and generosity of others until years, if not decades, later. My suggestion is if there is someone in your life that you recognize helped you, don't waste any time. Find them and thank them as soon as possible. If there was a teacher that made a lasting impact on your life, find their address and mail them a letter. Let them know what they taught you, how it improved your life, and where you are today. You have no idea the healing power such a note has for both the giver and the receiver. If the person you'd like to thank is no longer alive, then here's your chance to pay it forward. Think of how this person helped you and impacted your life, and then think of someone for whom you can do the same. Perhaps you were mentored as a young man or woman—and taught valuable lessons. Is there someone you can pass those lessons on to, thus making sure they are not lost from this world?

And when you do share those lessons, be sure to credit the person who taught you them. Tell those you're teaching about the person you so admired. Passing on another's legacy is such a powerful message to the universe. Ask for nothing in return. Don't even ask the person you're helping to pay it forward. *Show* them, don't tell them, how generosity works. I have no doubt that they, in turn, will pay it forward in their own time. In addition to paying it forward in service and gratitude, if you are able, donate money to causes that helped you along the way. I would be nothing without strong mentors, so I donate to the Girls and Boys Club of America because it's an organization built on the idea that a mentor can change a person's life.

If you're still not convinced of the power of gratitude and giving back, I suggest you try it for a week or two and see how dramatically your life changes. I believe nothing has the power to awaken your soul, align your purpose, or show you what you're meant to do like becoming a grateful and generous person. When you can feel compassion for others, recognize your own good fortune, and let go of your own hang-ups and complaints, you begin to realize that you are not the center of the universe. That's not to say you're not important. Rather, it's to say that your story and ever-unfolding drama here on Earth is no more important than any other's. It also means you can become part of the solution rather than the problem when you get out and help others. Believe me, the world needs more problem solvers, more givers, more compassionate people who are willing to do what others who are mired in their own suffering cannot.

And you don't have to pontificate or shout it from the rooftops that you're such a generous person if you're trying to get others to be generous too. What I have learned is you will be more likely to convince a person with your actions rather than your words. Writing this book is just one way to reach people. However, the most effective way I have found to make a lasting impact on others is by doing good works. One of my favorite sayings, commonly attributed to John Wesley, is: "Do all the good you can, by all means you can, in all the ways you can, in all the places you can, at all the times you can, to all the people you can, as long as you can." I can think of no better legacy in life than to succeed in doing such things. You'll not only live a good life; you'll help others to do so as well.

Stand up for what is right

Voltaire wisely said, "Every man is guilty of all the good he didn't do." When you're examining your life, it is easy to recall the injustices that have been done to you. But rarely do we stop and think of the injustices or injury we have caused others. And sometimes, it's what we failed to do that is the most harmful of all. When we don't stand up for what is right; when we don't do the kind thing; when we fail to act in a way that makes another's life easier or better, we miss the opportunity to be kind.

Saying you're sorry is difficult for some people, but it's the first and most noble step. Making amends or atoning for the mistake or harm is the next. Recognizing our human fallibility, weakness, and imperfections knocks us off the pedestal we put ourselves on. It's impossible to feel self-righteous or indignant when we admit that we are imperfect as well. It's easier to forgive and move on from harm done to us when we realize that we also may be in need of some forgiveness. We're all going to dance on our dance partners' toes. We're all going forget the steps and disappoint them too. The key is to say you're sorry, try your best to not do it again, and just keep dancing.

Giving money, giving our time, giving our kindness, and

for*giving* are generous acts that not only help *us* grow and heal—they also help the world. All around us there is poverty, disease, suffering, and loss. For some of us, it is hard to imagine just how destitute others are. We are so desensitized by what we see on the nightly news that it barely registers when we see a starving or sick child. Many of us haven't seen the level of poverty that exists around the world (and is sometimes closer than you think), but I have traveled to many countries—Germany, England, Italy, Spain, France, Monaco, Netherlands, Greece, Turkey, Belgium, Croatia, Switzerland, Estonia, Russia, Denmark, Finland, Czech Republic, Austria, Poland, Hungary, Mexico, Brazil, Argentina, Chile, Costa Rico, Panama, Cuba, Puerto Rico, Martinique, U.S. Virgin Islands, St. Thomas, St. Croix, Uruguay, Chile, Japan, South Korea, Japan, Canada, and all of the United States—and I can personally attest that there are people in such great need that it would bring most of us to our knees if we were in similar conditions. While it's important to give to causes that we're personally invested in or have been affected by, I would be remiss if I didn't encourage others to look beyond their own experience and learn as much as they can about others around the globe who may benefit from their help.

I don't have any personal connection to Mecca, California, but when I saw the conditions that many of these children were living in and going to school in, I couldn't help but reach out. There are an estimated 60 million people on this planet right now who don't have access to clean water. Our oceans are filling up with plastic. There is war and famine in many parts of the world. There are animals facing extinction. There are small children suffering from cancer. Even if none of these issues personally affect you, you can make a difference—even a small one—that can personally affect someone you will never meet.

Another aspect of giving back to the world that most of us don't think about is considering our own use of material items. We can all do small things every day that can make a big difference. We are such a consumer-based society—we think we have to buy more, more, more. But *not buying* things and instead reusing things and cutting back on our consumption of natural resources is something everyone can do, regardless of their socioeconomic status. Imagine the change we could all make if we are just a bit more conscious and aware of our individual impact in the world.

For me, being able to spend time with people I love and my friends is more important than anything I could do, and being able to dance and feel the rhythm of music is the most vital and important part of my life. Life is a precious gift, and looking back, I can say with authority that it goes by fast. If you don't take advantage of every minute of every day and you're not mindful of how you spend your time and resources, you might wake up one day and wonder: *Where did my life go? How did it all just vanish?* Being mindful, joyful, grateful, aligning your values, and giving back to the world as much as you can, while you can, is the surest way to guarantee that you won't look back on your life and feel like you have wasted one minute of it.

I hope by now you feel inspired to give—whatever you can. I can't think of a better way to spend your life. It's never too late to give, to look back and feel gratitude, to make amends, and to pay it forward. If you're alive, there is still time to make a difference and touch others. It's never too late to grow as a person.

And if nothing else, I can say with absolute authority that giving is great for the heart—for our entire health and well-being. When you give, you feel better. It's nearly impossible to feel stressed out when you're in a state of gratitude. Gratitude does the body good. If your health and well-being matter to you, let that be the incentive you need to volunteer, donate, or be generous in spirit.

I believe we are natural givers. This is what we were born to be and do. Somewhere along the line, we forgot how to do this, or we were treated badly and became bitter or hard-hearted. It's never too late to be who you want to be. At the end of your life, you will not be counting your dollars, but you can count your blessings. You will remember all the family, friends, and loved ones who helped you and who you helped.

We all want to feel that we have contributed, and we all want to make a mark on the world. If we have lived well, we have left the world a little bit better than how we found it. We don't have to be millionaires, famous, or Nobel Prize winners to make our mark. If we made someone else's life happier, if we used our skills and talents to help others, if we've helped someone accomplish a lifelong goal, if we've given to causes and organizations that will continue to make a difference long after we're gone, we have done what we were meant to do.

You have danced the dance. You can bow to your partner, knowing you have given it your all, and you can leave your mark on your corner of the dance floor before the lights go down.

EXERCISES THAT CAN HELP YOU GIVE BACK

- What gift or talent do you possess that can contribute to the happiness and joy of others?

- Who are you most grateful for in your life? What have these people given to you or made you realize?

- If they have passed on, how might you honor their memory or spirit?

- What ways can you pay it forward?

- What parts of your life have you been approaching with a scarcity mind-set? How can you begin to let that go and begin to give?

- Can you think of a time when you have been harsh to others? Is there any space in your heart for forgiveness?

- What areas of world need could you investigate a bit more? Could you see yourself giving to causes that you haven't considered in the past?

- What is the legacy you would like to leave behind? How do you plan on doing this?

CHAPTER 8

Dancing in the Rain

"Life isn't about waiting for the storm to be over; it's about learning how to dance in the rain."

—Vivian Green

In life, there will invariably be obstacles and challenges. I see these not as hardships but as *opportunities*, which should never hinder a person from attempting to achieve their goals and dreams. I have yet to meet an obstacle that I didn't approach with enthusiasm or the belief that I could overcome it—and if not overcome it, then at the very least learn from it. I have hiked Mount Everest to base camp—it took two weeks because we had to stop and acclimate every other day. I have hiked to the summit of many of Colorado's 14,000-foot peaks. I have done things in life I could never have dreamed possible when I was a boy on a farm. With each obstacle, you can discover unknown resources of strength, wisdom, and resolve. All you need to do is change how you think of the challenge and identify the humor—and hope—in each situation.

I encountered my first obstacle when I was very young. I was outside playing with friends. While running back from an outhouse, I didn't see a barbed wire fence, and I ran right into it. My face was caught on one of the razor-sharp barbs and instantly torn. All around me, it suddenly went very dark. I must have passed out, because when I woke up, I was on the ground, covered in blood. I reached up and felt my face, which was torn open completely from my mouth all the way through my cheek to my ear.

I got up and started running toward the house. My mother, obviously horrified, ran and got cold, wet towels to wrap my face. My father started the car. My mother picked me up and held me tightly in the back seat, applying pressure to my wrapped face. As a father myself, I can only imagine their fear. My father drove very fast and sped through many red lights. He was hoping a police officer would find him, so he could explain the situation and get safe passage for us to the hospital, but no police officers were in sight.

I remember arriving at the hospital and hearing the staff assure me I was going to be all right and they would take care of me. For some reason, I believed them. And lucky for me, the surgeon on call that night had just returned from Europe. He had served in the army and knew just what to do.

All in all, it took three different surgeries to sew my face back together and eventually fix the long scar that stretched from my mouth to my ear.

After the surgeries, I remember lying in bed all alone. My parents couldn't be with me the entire time I was in the hospital. I remember crying and being very scared and wanting my mother. At one point, I even got sick all over myself and the nurses had to come in and clean me up. It was a lonely and scary time. But throughout it all, I had this feeling that I was *okay*. The nurses assured me over and over I was *okay—and that I was lucky*.

It's hard to imagine how lucky you would feel, having your face split open and disfigured, but the more I've thought about it over the years, the more I've come to realize how right those nurses were. If I had been two inches shorter, the barbed wire would have blinded me. If I had been two inches taller, it would have been my throat that was ripped open. As long as I was alive, I was going to be okay.

Reframe the obstacles

Reframing obstacles is how we get miracles. When we look at problems and obstacles and only choose to see what is *wrong*, we can't see the other alternatives or the infinite possibilities that abound if we choose to think differently.

What was at first an obstacle for me became one of my greatest life lessons. I learned from an early age to tell myself that everything was going to be okay. Those nurses taught me to calm myself down and see that there was nothing to be afraid of, and I wasn't alone, because I had them. This experience also taught me that scars aren't something to be ashamed of. They make us who we are. They serve as reminders that we didn't succumb to life's challenges; we survived and overcame them.

All around us, people are there to help us overcome life's obstacles. When I was a child, I had my parents and then the nurses. I also had trusted friends and encouraging people all along the way. When I was in the army, I had mentors who pushed me further. In Eagle, Colorado, I had Leo Hargrave, who believed in me and taught me how to think and reason, and who didn't let the seemingly impossible stop me from doing anything. And, of course, I had my spiritual guides—the still, soft voices inside me that always knew just what to do if I asked them for their help and guidance.

It's more than luck

Throughout my life, I have wondered many times about my own success and my ability to overcome things that seem to undo most other people—poor education, limited resources, life-threatening injuries, the loss of a dear loved one, major financial obstacles in business. And I find myself asking: *How did that even happen? How did I get through that? Was I just really lucky?* But I think it's more than luck. Every one of us is going to be faced with obstacles and roadblocks and unforeseen accidents and heartbreaks along the way in life. It's how we react that truly separates those who are perceived as lucky from those with bad luck.

I can recall a time later in my career when, after I had become successful in the commercial laundry business, I thought I would go into purchasing apartments. At one point, I owned 200. One day a tenant came to me and said he'd like to go in 50/50 on buying a shopping center. I instantly said yes. Though I had no experience in owning retail shopping centers, I thought the opportunity sounded worthwhile. Well, at some point in the process, my 50/50 partner backed out—I suppose because he couldn't go through with accepting the risk. At that point, I had to make a choice: I could step away, too, and simply acknowledge this as an obstacle I couldn't overcome—or I could go through with it.

I went forward with the deal alone. And it was hugely successful.

What some see as luck, I see as persistence—a belief in myself and my God-given capabilities, a belief that everything can be improved, and that there is no problem too big or too complex that it can't be solved. Lucky people are grateful people. They are surrounded by good friends and mentors. They show up each day and do what needs to be done. More than anything, they share a fundamental belief that it will all be okay. To be a lucky person, you have to be positive and believe everything can and will work out for the best in the end.

To be a lucky person, you have to be positive and believe everything can and will work out for the best in the end.

Now, it's true that there was an element of luck in my child-hood accident. As I said, had I been any taller or shorter, my life today would have been radically different—or I would have no life at all. It's true that in that case I got lucky. But after that, I made my own luck. Instead of being a victim of my own circum-stance or allowing myself to be babied or even becoming fearful, I decided on a different route in life. I decided to let that accident make me smarter and more aware. I didn't let fear stop me from going out and running around with my friends. I also discovered a strength and resilience in myself that I would not otherwise have been aware of.

We need obstacles to overcome

So often in life, especially now, people around us want to protect us from our obstacles. We have parents who want to immediately fix things. But when we don't let children face obstacles head-on, we rob them of the ability to become strong and to see what they are made of. We rob them of the confidence and self-esteem that is earned from hard-fought battles.

I would not wish for a life without obstacles. Had I not had the ones I experienced from a young age, I know I would not be the man I am today. I know I wouldn't have had the strength and confidence that everything would be okay if I just stayed the course.

Every obstacle and every seemingly impossible moment in my life taught me something about myself and the world. When we look at our past through the lens of what we have learned instead of how we failed or how unlucky we were, we open ourselves up to amazing opportunities.

Furthermore, when we're not preoccupied with blaming our life's circumstances for our lot in life, we can get busy looking for solutions, asking questions, and seeking experts, mentors, spiritual guides, and others who can help us.

Life isn't going to be without losses, heartbreaks, or challenges. But each of them is simply a new path to self-discovery and an opportunity to be grateful for what one has. Being grateful for all things—both the good and bad—is the key to being able to persevere through life's greatest ordeals and heartbreaks.

> Being grateful for all things—both the good and bad—is the key to being able to persevere through life's greatest ordeals and heartbreaks.

We are all just seeds pushing through the earth's surface—we can't enjoy the gorgeous warmth of the sun and all the freedom of life if we don't do the hard work of pushing through the mud. So the next time life gets you down, something doesn't go your way, or someone fails to do something they promised, instead of throwing your arms up in resignation or despair, stop. Calm yourself down. Tell yourself it's all going to be okay. Reach out for help from friends, mentors, or spiritual guides, and welcome their help. Together, think of possible solutions. Then, instead of focusing on the problem, focus on positive outcomes. Most importantly, be sure to reframe the problem as a life lesson. If you do all these things, I promise you will never wait for a storm to pass again—you will have learned how to dance in the rain.

 EXERCISES THAT CAN HELP YOU OVERCOME ANY OBSTACLE

- What obstacles are you using as an excuse to hold you back from the life you imagine for yourself?

- Are these really impossible obstacles? List them and then write out possible ways to overcome them.

- What stories in your past have you held on to as excuses or reasons for your own bad luck?

- Is there a way you can reframe these obstacles? What are they teaching you about life? About yourself?

- Can you look back on any obstacles and observe any opportunities or positive outcomes that resulted from them?

- What obstacles are you grateful for? How has this challenge pointed out something you once took for granted?

CHAPTER 9

Shut Up and Dance

"There are those who dance to the rhythm that is played to them, those who only dance to their own rhythm, and those who don't dance at all."

—Jose Bergamin

Not many people like to hear this, but there comes a time in everyone's life when you have stop reading, stop talking, and *just fucking do it*. This is my go-to mantra. At some point, you have to take the first step and do it already.

I can say this with some authority: Life goes by fast, and there's no time to play around. There comes a time when you have to stop standing around, get on the dance floor, and show the world your moves. If the music is on—which is to say, *if you're still alive*—you should be out on that dance floor, dancing. Stop wasting your precious time. But don't despair if you're showing up late to the party. It's never too late to start something. I hope to be trying new things and starting new things until I take my dying breath. There is no guarantee for any of us in life. We can't take any moment for granted, and we need to come at life with a sense of urgency. Otherwise it will just pass us by.

Shut up and dance

There comes a time when you have to stop thinking about what you want to do—and just do it. There comes a time when you need to forget the obstacles and challenges, draw on your inner strength and resolve, take a chance, and just go. The greatest risk in life is not doing what we're meant to do and instead living a life of mediocrity. Who wants that? At some point, we all just have to just shut up and dance. In order to do so, however, you must surround yourself with positive, encouraging people—those who will hold you accountable.

> The greatest risk in life is not doing what we're meant to do and instead living a life of mediocrity!

When I decided to take up piano, I didn't half-ass it. I set up five lessons a week with someone who would hold me accountable. I hired the best teacher there was—Jeeyoon Kim, an accomplished concert pianist. I made sure I was accountable to someone every day. I set up a routine so that I had to do the work—no excuses, no complaining, no negativity. I hired someone who was going to constantly encourage me and who would be positive and inspiring. And then I showed up and did the work.

Day in and day out, I show up to the piano and take it one note at a time, just as I did when I was learning how to dance. And let me tell you, it's not always easy. I have my moments when I want to be lazy. We all have within us that little self-destruct button that we want to push when things seem a little challenging and difficult. It would be so easy to avoid the gym, eat the junk food, skip the dance lesson, and take a nap or watch a mindless television show.

Go toward the feeling

But how do you feel after you avoid what you're meant to do? If you're like me, it can make you can feel pretty lousy. Conversely, by choosing to do the hard work, you'll feel fantastic afterward. Nothing feels quite so good as accomplishing something.

So why do we put off something that will ultimately make us feel good? Why do we resist our own best interests? What holds us back from doing what we should even when we know from past experience how good we'll feel once we do it?

I would venture to say the reason is a bit of fear tinged with a good dose of comfort. We all want to be comfortable. We want the temperature to be just so, our bed to feel just right, our lives predictable and easy. If you ask a psychologist or a psychiatrist why people do things they know will make them unhappy, the answer is that people gravitate to the *familiar*.

But we can't grow when we're comfortable. We can't feel like we've accomplished something if it's not difficult or we're not afraid—at least a little.

We can't grow when we're comfortable.

We have to welcome the discomfort and make friends with our fears—fear of failure, fear of not finishing, fear of not being good enough, fear of disappointing others and ourselves—and just do it anyway.

Here's the thing: We all know we will feel better if we eat healthier. We will feel better if we work out regularly. We will look better if we take care of ourselves. We will feel accomplished if we do what we set out to do. So that is what you need to focus on. Go toward the *feeling* of accomplishment and satisfaction and feeling good, whatever the feeling is that you long for. Know that you will feel better if you do what you say you're going to do. So often we get hung up on the work right in front of us. It's hard. It's a struggle. It's uncomfortable. I get that. And so we often *only* see those hard and uncomfortable things, and that's why it's so hard for us to move forward.

However, if you tell yourself, "I will feel fantastic after this work out, and I want to feel fantastic," you will more likely go and work out. If you know you'll feel a sense of accomplishment from doing a small task at home, like cleaning out a closet or a junk drawer, then focus, not on the tedium or annoyance of the task, but on the feeling of accomplishment that will result, and you're more likely to do it. In fact, if you focus on how good it will feel to be done instead of how hard it is to do, you may even forget how hard or uncomfortable something is while you're doing it. Your mind is a powerful thing. If you tell yourself, "This is fun. I am doing it! I can do it," your mind will believe you and your body will follow.

Give yourself a deadline

Another thing I found helpful in terms of motivation is to have an ironclad deadline. Training for a competition, a race, a match, or an event is always a great motivator. However, if you're doing something that doesn't have a built-in deadline, my recommendation is to set one for yourself. Give yourself a dire consequence if you miss it. Perhaps you can't go to the concert you were planning on attending or you can't buy yourself something you had your heart set on. My suggestion is to make sure someone else is involved. If you tell someone else what you're about to do, what the deadline is, and what the consequence would be for failure, they will hold you to it. And most importantly: Act as if your life depends on it, because it does!

This is your wake-up call: You aren't going to be around forever. For some reason, so many people act as though they are. They spend so much of their lives coming up with excuses for why they shouldn't be doing things that they miss out on the entire point of life—to spend your time here purposefully, doing what you love with the people you love, while you have the time to do it.

As we get older, it seems the days go by so much quicker, which is all the more reason to not waste any time. As long as the music is playing, you should be dancing. You only have one life, and you should live it with gusto.

 ## EXERCISES THAT CAN HELP YOU START RIGHT NOW

- What new, exciting thing can you start today?
- Go out and find an expert, a mentor, or even a friend who can hold you accountable. Then set up the routine and lessons so you can begin.
- What is the feeling you long for most? Peace? Love? Health? Wholeness? Happiness? Accomplishment?
- What is one thing you can do to help you achieve that feeling today—right now?
- What will be your life's biggest regret if you don't do it before you die? Why haven't you done anything about it? What perception, fear, or negative belief is holding you back?
- What is one thing you can do today so you don't die with any regrets?

Conclusion

"I want to dance. I want to live."

—Domenico Dolce

I don't need to be told how precious and short life is. Though I consider myself to be a strong and healthy person, I have had my share of health scares. Not long ago, I needed to have surgery to replace a heart valve. It was a necessary procedure and one I could hardly put off. I went in thinking only positively—that I would be okay and all would be well. I wanted to get my heart fixed and get back on the dance floor.

Well, there were some unforeseen complications during the surgery, and, long story short, I almost died.

While in recovery, my weight diminished. I had difficulty breathing, and eventually the doctors started to prepare my friends and family for the worst: I wasn't going to make it. My body just couldn't go on any longer. They didn't think I had the strength to fight my way back.

While these conversations were taking place, I was lying in

bed, and I started to believe these things myself. I thought, *Well, Allen, this is it. You're tired. You're weak. You can't beat this.*

Then suddenly something miraculous happened. My piano instructor, Jeeyoon, and my dance instructors all showed up at my bedside. Surrounding me with love and encouragement, they begged me to wake up and rally. They reminded me of my own words, and of all I had left to do in this life. Over and over they said, "Allen, we need you."

Let me tell you a little secret: The greatest and most powerful feeling in the world is the feeling of being needed. When others need us, love us, and want us around, it's incredibly powerful. It's— dare I say it—miraculously healing.

> The greatest and most powerful feeling in the world is the feeling of being needed.

I was needed. I had more work to do. I still had dance competitions to dance in, sonatas to learn, and books to write. I had glaciers to visit, mountains to climb, trips to take with children and grandchildren. I had an entire life waiting for me. All I had to do was show up and live it.

And I'll let you in on another little secret: The world needs you too. The world needs your unique talents, points of view, service, kindness, love, intelligence, and optimism. It needs people who are willing to do what needs to be done, who aren't afraid of obstacles, who are willing to do the impossible, and who go after what they want.

You have to dance until the last note is played, until your last life-giving force of breath leaves you and your soul moves on to the next dance floor that beckons it. You never know what is next. You can never know what surprises you will discover along the way when you open yourself to all the infinite possibilities of the universe. For example, when I set out on this quest to write a book, I hoped I would discover what it was that made me who I am and contributed to the amazing life I was able to lead. But what I discovered along the way showed me so much more.

In recalling my life, I saw how rich and complex it was and how so many amazing people, events, and books contributed to my success along the way. I didn't go through any of it alone. And most importantly, I discovered that my purpose was ultimately to share with others all that I had learned in this life. My story is your story. It's all of our stories. We can all overcome. We can all make our life into the stuff dreams are made of. All you have to do is remember the lessons I learned and which I now bequeath to you:

- You were born to do something great.
- You are a miracle machine.
- You have an untapped reservoir of strength, confidence, and resilience.
- You know instinctively what you need to do to succeed.
- You can accomplish more than you originally thought you could.
- You must stretch the limits of your imagination and get free of your current limiting environment and self-limiting thought patterns.

- The key to enjoying your life is to approach everything as a child—with a beginner's mind-set, a willingness to fail, and an intention to learn something new every day.

- You just need to believe that everything can be improved—even when you think you have reached your best, there is always something that can be made better or easier.

- If you want to succeed and achieve, you need to set goals.

- Surround yourselves with positive and encouraging role models and mentors.

- *Love* your obstacles and see them as opportunities for growth.

- Be willing to practice and take repetitive action to master each skill.

- Read and build a library of inspiring and forward-thinking books.

- Be flexible and open—willing to go with the flow.

- Know that what you can dream or imagine, you can create.

- Understand that the mind is more powerful than you know; what you think, you become.

- You can achieve the impossible. In fact, if it doesn't seem impossible, it's not worth pursuing.

- Avoid negativity, excuses, self-limiting behaviors, and people who want to hold you back. Get away from them as fast as possible.

- Be generous and grateful and give back whenever possible. Remember all the people who helped you along the way.

- Believe in yourself, and your life can be anything you want it to be.

- *Decide* to be happy and look for the good in everything—or look for how you can improve it.

- If your actions inspire and enable others to dream more, learn more, do more, and become more, then you have truly succeeded.

- And finally, if all else fails: Just dance.

Allen's Library of Forward-Thinking Books

How to Win Friends and Influence People, Dale Carnegie, Simon and Schuster, 1936

Secrets of a Millionaire Mind, T. Harv Eker, Harper Business, 2005

Outliers: The Story of Success, Malcolm Gladwell, Little Brown, 2008

You Can Heal Your Life, Louise Hay, Hay House, 1984

Think and Grow Rich, Napoleon Hill, The Ralston Society, 1937

Success Through a Positive Mental Attitude, Napoleon Hill, HarperCollins, 1961

Rich Dad, Poor Dad, Robert T. Kiyosaki, Warner Books, 2000

The Power of Positive Thinking, Norman Vincent Peale, Prentice-Hall, 1952

Elite Minds: How Winners Think Differently to Create a

Competitive Edge and Maximize Success, Stan Beecham, McGraw-Hill Education, 2016

Hit Refresh: The Quest to Rediscover Microsoft's Soul and Imagine a Better Future, Satya Nadella, HarperBusiness, 2017

About the Author

Allen T. Brown began his education when he was 17. He climbed aboard a freighter transporting iron ore from Canada to Chicago. Attachments to friends and relatives were severed and freedoms soon revealed themselves.

After his experience on the freighter, Allen became even more curious about what the world had to offer, so he joined the Army. As a soldier, he spent time in Germany and made many new friends who encouraged him to read and study, which eventually led him to attend college. After graduating from the University of Michigan with a bachelor's degree in literature, he moved to Colorado and became headmaster of Vail Country Day School.

At the time, Vail was just beginning to become the popular skiing and vacation hamlet it is today, and Allen was surrounded by builders. One day, he heard one of the developers say, "I will have the law changed if it interferes with what we need to do." From this statement grew an understanding that we have many options.

Allen made his fortune in Vail and California, turning $12.00 into $30 million. He maintains shopping centers in California and Colorado.

Allen never ceases growing and continues his education to this day, from becoming one of the top amateur ballroom dancers to learning classical piano. He maintains the courage to be curious, and of course the courage to act on that curiosity. He feels that only the impossible is worthy of his time and mind.